Love God Get High

LIVING UNDER THE INFLUENCE

Love God Get High

LIVING UNDER THE INFLUENCE

MIKE MOORE

Library of Congress Control Number: 2023910101

ISBN: 978-1-956065-13-8

Published by EDK Books & Distribution, LLC
www.edkbooksanddistribution.com

Cover design by Julie K. Lee/Lee Creative
jkleecreative@gmail.com

Contents

FOREWORD BY PETER LOUIS

HAVE YOU EVER FELT LIKE something is missing in your life? Or rather . . . *someone* is missing? Well the truth is . . . there is *Someone* missing. You weren't created to get through life all by yourself. You weren't made to just keep grinding day after day in your own strength until you get your break. *You need help!* And the good news is there is *Someone* whose very delight is to help you!

The most famous, most beautiful, and most sought-after person in all of history, Jesus Christ, told His friends and followers that it is better for Him to leave their presence than to stay with them! He goes on to explain that if He leaves, He will send another, *the Helper*, to be with them forever. And this Helper, the Holy Spirit, is the most wonderful subject of this timely book.

Believe it or not, you were created to be the recipient of God's daily divine help. And His gracious help comes to us through this Helper in the form of unconditional love, limitless joy, and unending peace! I don't think it is an overstatement to say that cultivating a real, experiential relationship with the Holy Spirit is the most important pursuit anyone could make.

I'm so thankful for Mike's voice and the wealth of spiritual truth he brings to light in this book. I've known Mike Moore for many years, and the only thing that rivals his passion for God is his desire to see other people encounter God in a very real way.

And how can anyone encounter the Father and the Son except by the Holy Spirit? In this book, Mike will provoke you to want to know the Holy Spirit for yourself, to ask the questions you've always wanted to ask, and then to help you answer them by giving you practical biblical truths that will ultimately deepen your relationship with the Holy Spirit.

May God use this book to help every believer learn to live under the influence of God's magnificent Holy Spirit!

Peter Louis
Braveheart Ministries
www.braveheart318.com
www.linkedin.com/in/plouis

ACKNOWLEDGEMENTS

Whom to acknowledge? Since this is my fourth book and my life has been so blessed with many friends, family members, and business associates . . . whom do I choose? I would need this book to list them all!

So I want to ACKNOWLEDGE the Holy Spirit, who Jesus graciously sent to us after His resurrection and whom we receive after acknowledging JESUS as Savior and LORD!! Thank you!!!

Introduction

IF YOU ARE NOT HIGH in the Holy Spirit, you can't fully experience God. Unlike a temporary emotional (or drug-induced) high, a Holy Spirit high is meant to be ongoing . . . like joy. The Book of Wisdom, AKA **Proverbs 15**, says: "All the days of the oppressed are wretched, but the cheerful heart [of joy] has a continual feast." That's what living under the influence of the Holy Spirit is like (an each-day journey, not dependent on circumstances).

This book gets its vision from the Gospel of **John 14** (English Standard Version): "I will ask the Father, and he will give you another Helper, to be with you forever, even the Spirit of truth, whom the world cannot receive, because it neither sees him nor knows him. You know him, for he dwells with you and will be in you." Everybody, are you listening to this? God gave us His Holy Spirit! Not only is He in us (who believe); He also dwells with us and promises to stay FOREVER.

He's in us! He's not walking away from us.

And that Spirit, who dwells with us and abides with us forever, is the same Spirit that raised Jesus from the dead. That's the Power that dwells within us. How can we neglect to understand who this amazing part of the Godhead is?

Lord willing, this book, with all its Dares and Prayers, will bring us to a deeper understanding of Who the Spirit is.

Why don't we say: "Holy Spirit, open my eyes. Holy Spirit, fill me (today) with such a deep understanding of who You are in me that I can experience and share Your abiding love"?

This book is dedicated to the inerrancy of Scripture and the three-fold nature of God, called the Trinity, which is consistent with the Shema in **Deuteronomy 6**: "Hear, O Israel: The LORD our God is one LORD." (King James Version)

That truth is also settled in **1 John 5**, "For there are three that bear witness in heaven, the Father, the Word, and the Holy Ghost; and these three are one." (NKJV) The Word, of course, is Jesus, and He makes provision for us to walk in the Spirit of God, doing the works of God, by the power of God.

Your Spirit-led walk awaits . . .

Mike

Part 1

FIND YOUR SUPPLIER

1

FATHER, SON, AND . . .

MOST CHURCHES BELIEVE in the Trinity. However, if you really pay attention to what's preached, you realize that it's the Father, the Son, and the *Holy Bible*. Those churches solely focus on the Father and the Son, but they're really big in the Holy Bible (and that is awesome), but the Holy Spirit gets short shrift.

Without malice (on their part), they're splitting Jesus and the Word of God, where Jesus *is* the Word. If you want to be more correct, the Trinity is the Father, the Word of God, and the Holy Spirit. The Word of God is Jesus. (**Revelation 19**) But so often we're missing the Holy Spirit.

What is the role of the Holy Spirit?

How does He work in our day-to-day life?

Do we pray to Him?

Should we honor Him and worship Him?

These are questions that (more often than not) go unanswered but are addressed throughout this book because fellowship in (or with) the Spirit is so important that Jesus kept His followers in Jerusalem until they were baptized with (or in) the Holy Spirit.

If we look at **John 16**, Jesus is saying: "It's beneficial for you that I go, for if I go, I'll send another Helper, the Holy Spirit, who is the Spirit of truth. He will guide you in all things that I have taught you." We see the Holy Spirit is going to bring to remembrance everything that the Word says. Without the Holy Spirit, we're not able to really understand, grasp, or lay hold to the Word of God.

The Holy Spirit's job is to bring honor and glory to the Lord Jesus. He's pointing us to Jesus. The Holy Spirit is our helper. Let's remember, in the **Book of Genesis**, that Abraham had a servant named Eliezer. What I find notable is that Eliezer, in the original Hebrew, means *helper*.

Abraham was the father of us all. In **Genesis 24**, we learn he sent his key servant out (the helper/Holy Spirit) to go find a bride for Isaac (his son). There's the Trinity right there: You had the father (Abraham), the son (Isaac), and the helper/Holy Spirit (Eliezer). Eliezer traveled 450 miles and found a bride (Rebekah) for the son.[1]

Is that not one of the roles of the Holy Spirit? He goes out and finds the one and only bride for Jesus.

---

[1] Of course, Mercedes Benz was not an option back then. Camels travel at 3mph. That's 36 miles a day, or 12 days, to go 450 miles.

God's bride for Isaac was not where Isaac and Abraham lived. Therefore, the servant/helper had to go to another land to fetch just the right bride for Isaac.

Get this: Jesus was with His Father in Heaven. His bride was not to be found there. The bride was on Earth. *Who is the bride?* WE are the bride! Conversely, Adam's bride was not in Heaven either. God made him a bride on Earth (Eve). In both cases, God supplied an earthly bride.

In Isaac's case, God brought Rebekah to him. In Jesus's case, the Holy Spirit brought the BRIDEGROOM to the bride. *How?* When the Holy Spirit caused Mary to conceive Jesus in her womb. That is revealed in the **first chapter of Matthew**. Ever since Jesus became the bridegroom, the Holy Spirit has actively pursued the lost to become a part of the bride of Christ.

There is another key role of the Holy Spirit. The Word of God tells us that the Holy Spirit is the One (according to **John 16**) that convicts us of three things, *sin, righteousness, and judgment*: (1) of sin "because they don't know Me," (2) of righteousness "because I go to the Father," and (3) of judgment "because the ruler of the world is judged." *Convict*, in the Greek, is also the word *convince*. (G1651[2])

---

[2] Strong's Exhaustive Concordance notation for the Greek translation.

The word *convict*, today, has a different meaning. We think of that word as *he's convicted of a crime* or *he did something wrong*. To convince, however, is to show you enough facts that you're "won over" or "persuaded" of something to be a truth.

John 16 says: "will convict the world." (New King James Version) Let's stop there. *Who's in the world?* Believers, non-believers, and the demonic. They're all in the world today. The **gospel of John** says: "He will reprove [or convince] the world of sin . . . because they believe not on Me." (KJV) So obviously, they're non-believers, or what I refer to as "pre-believers." They don't believe in Jesus.

Thus, the role of the Holy Spirit (towards pre-believers) is to convince them that Jesus died on a cross for their sin and that (without Him) they will never gain eternal life because He's the only One where forgiveness of our sin is possible.

Who else is in the world? It says: "He will convict the world . . . of righteousness, because I go to My Father, and you see Me no more." (NKJV) *Who are those folks— who will see Him no more?* The people that already believed in Him; those are the followers of Jesus. The Holy Spirit's not convicting them of sin; they've already been convinced of sin in their life. When we came to Jesus, the Word says: "Their sins and their lawless deeds I will remember no more." (**Hebrews 10**, NKJV)

Once a person comes to Christ, Holy Spirit's ongoing job is to convince believers of their *right standing in Christ.* Everybody, He's convincing you of your right standing. He's saying: *Do you know who you are? You're in right standing with the Father. You're the child of the Most High God. You make mistakes, but that's not who you are. That's not what you do. People that are in right standing don't continually do that behavior; but if that happens, you're forgiven already. Knowing you're forgiven already will keep you from doing that behavior in the future.*

Last, He convicts the enemy (who is the prince of the power of the air, the demonic) that they're already judged. They'll never have a chance to be otherwise.

Let's add something about what the demonic tries to do to believers. He's accusing you and condemning you, but we are not condemned anymore. Consider **Romans 8:1**: "There is now no condemnation for those who are in Christ," but when we sin, or get into a habit of sin, the enemy wants to say: "See, you're not a believer." He tries to tell us that, but he can't because we are believers. No, he wants to convince you that you're condemned. (That's the very opposite to what the Holy Spirit says.)

The Holy Spirit's response to that accusation is to remind us: *You're still in right standing.* When we sin, **1**

John 2 assures us that Jesus, Himself, is advocating for us before the Father.

Therefore, when you go from pre-believer to believer, you're already free. You're completely free! You can choose freedom every day because you're in a new establishment that serves freedom 24/7/365. Let's choose to be freedom-conscious and forgiveness-conscious, not sin-conscious and bondage-conscious.

That freedom awareness/consciousness is not dependent on feeling the Holy Spirit. For sure, at times, you may feel the Holy Spirit. But listen, we will be talking later about being sealed. You may not feel sealed, but that doesn't mean you're not sealed.

At times, I may not feel forgiven, but I am forgiven. Just because I don't feel it doesn't mean I'm not forgiven. Just because we don't feel the presence of the Holy Spirit, or the presence of God, does not mean the presence of God is not with us. There are times I feel His palpable presence. There are times I can feel the power of God (privately or corporately), yet that doesn't mean if I don't feel it, the power of God's not with me.

You may not know it, but I'm half-Italian and half-Irish. When I'm with my Italian relatives, eating Italian food, drinking Italian wine, and enjoying Italian meatballs with red sauce, I'm at the table with people that speak Italian. When I'm with that side of the family, I feel Italian. But when I'm walking around Dallas, Texas, I may not feel Italian. That doesn't mean I'm not Italian.

I DARE YOU to focus on the evidence of the Holy Spirit in your life, not feelings. *What evidence?* Love, joy, peace, forbearance, kindness, goodness, faithfulness, gentleness, and self-control.

> "The fruit of the Spirit is fundamentally relational. Rather than originating with us, it flows to us from our union with Christ, and it flows beyond us to bring us into fellowship with others. The secret of this flow—and our unity with God and others—is humility."
> **– Jerry Bridges**

> *Do not get drunk on wine, which leads to debauchery. Instead, be filled with the Spirit.*
> **– Ephesians 5:18**

May God use this book to help you lead a life filled with the Spirit.

REMINDER: We are not victims of our circumstances; children are. We, as adults, are victims of our choices. *Choose wisely. Choose Holy Spirit.*

2

ESPECIALLY FOR YOU

THIS BOOK IS WRITTEN to believers and pre-believers. *What are pre-believers?* Whether they realize it or not, they're people still seeking to understand that Jesus is the Way, the Truth, and the Life; those who do not know that Jesus Christ died on His cross for their sins.

The Holy Spirit is like Eliezer, the servant who went out to find a bride for Isaac. We talked about him in the last chapter. If you are a pre-believer, the Holy Spirit has faithfully been out looking for *you*. Maybe you're feeling it, maybe you're not, but Jesus is standing at the door (of your heart) knocking. Whoever opens the door, He will come in and bless you from the inside out. (**Revelation 3**)

Are you fed up with life because everything seems to be working against you? Maybe life's overwhelming you in the areas of work, relationships, finances, past failures, dumpster-fire religious experiences, addictions, or destructive habits.

Plus, there are often nagging questions: *What's the purpose of this life? Is there something better?* As far as your pride goes, you now realize it offers you nothing. Deep in your heart, you're feeling a need to look at God's face and say: "*Why not me, why not now?*"

Friends, all Christian believers you know (and all you don't know) have faced those kinds of questions. Maybe things were going so well without God . . . until they weren't. Then it all went to Hell-in-a-handbasket. Maybe a beloved friend or relative died and they were faced with the inevitability of death and the afterlife. Maybe they got sick and God miraculously healed them, or they had some other undeniable God-thing happen to them to cause their selfish world to be turned upside down and shaken. *The path to God is a path of brokenness.*

Years ago, a nineteen-year-old young woman saw Jesus at the very lowest time in her life. She was a "believer all her life" but was bedridden, suffering, and gradually dying of advanced fibromyalgia. At the depth of her helplessness and discouragement, Jesus came to her as she was saying, "I can't do this. I can't do this! I need You now because I can't deal with this!"

Her eyes were closed, but she saw Jesus walk up to her. She continues: "He showed me His hands and the holes [in them]. There was still blood in the holes of His hands. I asked, 'Why is there blood in your hands?' and

He said, 'To show Satan because that's the payment. That's the payment for everything.' He turned around and lifted up His tunic to show me His back." [Folks, stay with this to the end.]

"You know how it says, 'By His stripes we are healed'?" [**Isaiah 53** and **1 Peter 2**] They didn't seem like stripes to Niki. She described them as gashes: "They were [over an inch] wide and very deep. You don't mend from something like that . . . they were slightly scarred over and they were all over [His back]. He was brutalized . . . He was tortured.

"This was the kicker for me. He turned around and He leaned in real close to me. [I saw] one cheekbone was higher than the other, and there was so much scar tissue around His eyes that you could barely see His eyes, but you could see 'em because the Word says He was beaten beyond recognition. [**Isaiah 53**] How are you recognized but by your face? I had never thought of that!

"I've known God all my life, and you think that when you get to Heaven, you'll see His scars and His hands but never about His face. And it broke my heart because my best Friend was standing in front of me saying, 'I did this for you because I love you.' He didn't stand in front of me to say 'Why aren't you trusting Me? Why are you flipping out right now?' He stood in front of me to say 'Look what I did. It's done, Niki. You're going to be healed. I've already paid for it.' He said, 'I love you,' and I said, 'I love you too.'" Niki Ochenski did survive and was healed entirely!

I mention the outcome of her experience only because you were wondering about it, but we are reading her account because she was a broken believer. Unlike most people, her brokenness didn't come by guilt and shame. It came by revelation of the depth of Jesus's *suffering body* as a once-and-for-all substitute for the sufferings of our bodies. Out of which His *shed blood* paid for our past, present, and future sins. You heard her say: "It broke my heart."

Niki's story reveals to us that there is a difference between the road of brokenness and the road of despair. She was at the end of her rope, on the road of despair—leading to depression. Jesus had to pay her a visit to get her on the road to brokenness—leading to hope, security in Him, and faith for what was coming to her.

Yes, both involve tears. Both involve deep emotions. Please track with me on this crucial point. Despair focuses on *me*; brokenness focuses on *Him*. Niki's testimony is that you can't look into the mangled and disfigured face of Jesus and not be broken.

Now, before you evangelicals overanalyze this, we can agree that Jesus could have shown Niki His face at any point of His life: His baby face in a manger, His youthful face as He was in the temple when His folks were looking for Him. So (of course) He could show Niki His face at its worst. That is not the face of His present, glorified body. That is not the face that Mary Magdalene saw in the garden (**Mark 16**); that is not the face the two men saw as they were walking from Jerusalem to Emmaus. (**Luke 24**)

Jesus showed Niki the face *she needed to see* at that moment in her life, and it made all the difference! Seeing the face of Jesus will make a difference in all of us! *What do you see when you see Jesus? What face of Jesus is He showing you right now?* Let's join King David in saying to God: "Your face, Lord, will I seek." (**Psalm 27**)

Moses had such a desire for intimacy with God that he asked to see His face in **Exodus 33**. God told him that no man can see His face and live. Yet, we can look to Jesus and live. In fact, **Numbers 21** compels us to "look and live." *Look to Jesus and live.* As you read about God, the Holy Spirit, we know that He can bring us face-to-face with Jesus—any way He chooses, any way we need.

I DARE YOU to reflect on the moment(s) that you went from unbrokenness to brokenness. Brokenness is not just the loss of self-esteem, to be avoided. It is a pathway to true connecting with the Lord, to be embraced. Pride is your enemy. Brokenness is your friend.

"Jesus said: "Blessed are the poor in spirit"
—contrary to what we would expect,
brokenness is the pathway to blessing!
There are no alternative routes; there are no
shortcuts. The very thing we dread and are
tempted to resist is actually the means to
God's greatest blessing in our lives."
– Nancy Leigh DeMoss

My sacrifice, O God, is a broken spirit; a
broken and contrite heart you, God, will
not despise.
– Psalm 51:17

May you see the face of the Savior as you face real
challenges to your life and your faith.

REMINDER: We are not victims of our circumstances;
children are. We, as adults, are victims of our choices.
Choose wisely. Choose Holy Spirit.

3

BAGLESS IN MONTEREY

THE ORIGINAL DRAFT of chapter 3 of this book was a teaching chapter. I read it over, and God didn't give me a green light to use it. Instead, it has gone from a *teaching* chapter to a *testimony* chapter: real stories, involving real people. In both accounts you can see how the Holy Spirit acts like our spiritual thermostat. When we get cold and indifferent towards God, Holy Spirit warms us up. When we get too hot about ourselves, Holy Spirit cools us down.

In June of 2022, the company I work for hosted key sales staff to an *all-expense-paid* vacation in Pebble Beach, California. It is known for hosting major pro golf events, but since I'm an average golfer, I just consider Pebble Beach a fusion of elegance and stunning natural beauty. The beauty is in the forest and breathtaking beaches. The elegance is displayed in Pebble Beach's residences. Clint Eastwood's Hacienda Este Madera (House East Wood) was at 17 Mile, Pebble Beach at one time. Other former or current residents you may know are actor Gene Hackman, Charles Schwab, and former secretary of state Condoleezza Rice.

We left on this company trip Wednesday, June 29, and were to stay till the Fourth of July. I arrived in California Wednesday afternoon, but my luggage was delayed. The airline said it would likely arrive in the evening, but it never came. Next day, never came. I went to the Monterey airport and talked to an agent. He looked up my claim number and said it was scanned in Dallas and that's as far as it got.

So my company sent a guy who had all the information to the Dallas airport's baggage claim . . . nothing! They said the luggage was probably in Bag Central. Bag Central is not owned by an airline. It's a third-party receiver (from all the airlines) of bags that have limited means of identification. Our guy told me: "Chances are you'll never see it again."

So I'm well over one thousand miles from home without a bag; nothing but a T-shirt, a pair of jeans, and my shoes. No underwear to change into, no deodorant, no toothpaste, nada!

When I saw my boss, I said, "Look, I'm going to go home. I know the company paid a lot of money for this trip, but for me to go out and buy an entire wardrobe just to stay here defeats the purpose of the trip." He said, "You can't go home. You're one of our top guys."

Then he went from encourager to enforcer: "Mike, I'm not asking you; I'm telling you—you're not going home. Buy some clothing, incidentals, etc., and expense it!"

So, I went and did what he requested (demanded—LOL). Still didn't have my luggage, but I had enough clean clothes to get through each day.

Later, the CEO of the company heard what happened. He said to me, "Mike, fly home with me on my jet when I leave." I thanked him for his kind offer but told him, "I'm leaving the airport very early in the morning to get to DFW and figure out what happened to my bag." Folks, *I just wanted my clothing.* I had a serious investment in the clothing in my bag. I was not about to lose them.

So I leave Monday morning on a plane, and it's supposed to land around noon in Dallas.

Here's my prayer: "Lord, this request is a *tall order.* I'd love to go to baggage claim and find my bag next to the carousel, just sitting right there. I take it, and I go home. You know where it's at, so I'm just looking at you." That was my prayer, simple and heartfelt.

The plane lands and I get off. At this airport, each terminal (A-D) has three carousels: North, South, and Middle. When I departed Wednesday, I was in B-2 (South). I had just now landed at B-50 (that's North). So I go to the baggage claim after I get off. Obviously, I just have a carry-on with me.

I have all the info they need. Ahead of me is a lady from London with a disabled child. This woman was on fire: "Where's my wheelchair? I can't believe this! My son needs a wheelchair!" *Blah, blah, blah.* She turns and sees me standing there and says, "Sir, this is going to be awhile. I suggest you go somewhere else." I was taken aback and said, "OK, but may I ask him [the clerk] a question?" She said, "Nope, you can't! He's mine, and I'm going to be here a long time." I looked at her son and just nodded and then went outside. My Uber was there. In two minutes, we're at the middle section. It's closed off for repairs. We go to the end. That's when I remember that I originally checked in at B-2, and I walk in.

There're two baggage agents working the kiosk. The guy is taking care of an airline agent, and the gal is dealing with two guys that are trying to get to Shreveport, Louisiana. They want their luggage off the plane because they now want to drive there instead. She tries to tell them that they might not be able to retrieve the luggage if it is in the cargo hold, and *you'll be waiting and you'll miss your blah, blah, blah.* No one was getting satisfied with all this, and my Uber meter is running outside while this agent devotes her attention to this hopeless scenario. Finally, I ask the baggage gal if their bags were scanned. She says they were. So I look at the guys and say, "If it's scanned, it will be in there. I'm going through this right now." That seems to get through to them. They even say, "Better to hear that from a passenger than an airline staffer," and they leave.

That staffer says, "Thank you for doing that." I say, "Maybe you can help me," and I give her this sheet of paper with my baggage claim details. I say, "Is it in Bag Central? If I give somebody a wad of hundreds, would I be able to go in and look for my bag?" She says, "No, it's fifth-level security; you'd never get in. The CEO of [the airline] can't get in there because of security measures against bombs and all that stuff. But she adds, "Let me look online."

At this point, it's been five days since I checked that bag. *Do you remember my prayer?*

She looks up to me and remarks: "Tumi! Tumi Luggage. You have a blue ribbon around your handle." She excitedly says, "Sir, I touched your bag! I know this bag." I go, "Ma'am, you probably see a million bags a day." She insists, "I know you would think that, but that's an expensive bag. Less than 1 percent of the bags we see are Tumi. This description . . . I just feel like I know this bag. As a matter of fact, I think it's in this cabinet." She points *next to this carousel.* Kiddingly, she says, "So, you'll give me one hundred dollars if it is in there?" I say, "Ma'am, gladly!" She opens the cabinet up, and there's my bag with the blue ribbon sitting inside.

She says, "You have to show me you know what's in this bag. Be specific." I tell her a bottle of a certain brand of vitamins is inside, and she agrees that's specific enough and says (with a smile), "Take your bag." Before I pick up the bag, I pull out a hundred-dollar bill and hold it out to her. She says, "I can't take that from you." Now it is my turn to smile as I say, "It's not from me; it's from Jesus." She replies, "Based on that, I can accept it," and she starts crying (for joy). She must have needed that hundred dollars more than I knew!

Now let's pretend you are God's right-hand person and you hear Mike Moore's prayer (on his flight back to Dallas) to get his Tumi bag back. Would you:

- put an angry Brit ahead of him in the north terminal,

- close the middle terminal to get him to the south terminal, and

- use his Italian boldness to help out one (of two) baggage agents—who *happens* to remember handling his Tumi bag and can walk right to it . . . and it's next to the carousel, just like he prayed?

Are you tracking with me? God's purpose for me wasn't to lose my luggage and contents for good; it wasn't to fly in a private jet with the CEO; it wasn't to smooth things over with the guys driving to Louisiana. It was God using me to bless a woman that He loves and cares about! *He knew* I would have a hundred-dollar bill on me. *He knew* she worked in baggage claim (for this particular airline) and the only way I would meet her would be if I went to that South Terminal baggage claim—during her shift! *Hallelujah.*

When I got back into the Uber to go home, the Lord said to me, "Mike, I want My people to live their life (daily) with this kind of view towards Me: *I will guide you.*" And who does Father God use to guide us? His Holy Spirit!

Not two years ago, a friend of mine was attending a Christian health conference in Thomaston, Georgia. I'm not saying his name because I have to share his personal dental issue with you. Over the course of fifty-plus years, he had lost all bottom molars, so he needs to wear a partial denture thing. Without it, he cannot eat anything that needs chewing (which is about everything). No carrots or salad or steak; nothing. The partial was fairly new to him and a bit irritating to have on while his mouth learned to assimilate its presence over time, so he had a habit of taking it off for a breather when he could.

It was a sizzling summer day in Thomaston, and he had finished off a Chick-fil-A peach shake, and the empty cup was left in the cupholder of his rental car. The conference he attended was over for the day, and he needed to get to a Home Depot, on the other side of town, to buy a personal cooler (for packing lunches). On the drive there, he took off his partial and looked for a safe place to keep it for a while. Because it wasn't his personal car, most options seemed too gross, so he opted to set it on the clear plastic dome of the empty shake cup. In fact, he thought that was a clever (and reasonably sanitary) place.

Once he got to Home Depot, he spied a trash container in front of the store and realized the interior of the rental car had some debris here and there, so before he went into the store, he decided to tidy up the vehicle and deposit the accumulated trash as he walked in. He made fast work of the back and front of the car. With a bit of smug satisfaction, he was barely able to add his trash to the mostly full container.

He went in, bought his cooler, got in the car, and then drove to his cabin about twenty minutes away. It was getting dark when he arrived, and after he got inside, he realized he forgot to bring in his "teeth." He went back to the car and found that the cup was no longer there! He didn't remember taking it out, but he obviously did. It must have gone out with the other trash!

It was his second day of a two-week conference, two thousand miles from home, and a scary alternative reality flashed in his mind:

It's 8:45 p.m. The store closes at 9 p.m. It will take more than fifteen minutes to drive there. What if emp-

tying the trash is the first thing they do as their closing routine?

Followed by:

I may not be able to eat the rest of my time here. Once I get home, it will take at least a week to get fitted for a new partial. That's about a month without chewing food!

As this was beginning to scare the crap out of him, he realized those thoughts were hurting more than helping. Instead, he began to pray: "Lord, I can't get there before they close. PLEASE keep the Home Depot people from emptying that container until after I go through it!"

This was a desperate prayer of a guy desperate enough to rummage through the garbage container if he had to. His son was waiting for him in the cabin. After explaining what had happened, they took the fastest route back, but it didn't seem fast enough. Finally, they drove into the Home Depot parking lot at 9:12 and as close to the front as the parking spaces allowed. To his dismay, he couldn't even see the container! *Had they already taken the whole thing away?*

He got out of the car and walked quickly towards the front. Yay! The container was still there (it was obscured by an object in front of it). *But were the contents still inside?* There was a taped-up used baby diaper sitting on the rim of the container. He remembered seeing that (and being disgusted before), but it gave him some assurance that the contents weren't disturbed.

He peered inside and saw the shake cup! But There was nothing on the clear rim of it. Before panic attack #3 had time to set in, he looked inside the cup and found the partial denture nestled in the bottom. *Hallelujah!* What a relief!

His adult son was waiting for him in the car when he came back to announce the good news. On the way in, the son had spotted a Wendy's that was still open, and as they were about to drive off to get fuel, he reminded his dad that it was after nine o'clock and they hadn't had dinner yet. So they headed towards the drive thru.

They ordered and drove up to the pay window. There was a truck ahead of them at the pickup window as my friend paid for their meals. The truck was still there and didn't seem to be driving off soon, so my friend said to the young lady at the window, "My son and I are from [the West Coast], and we love Jesus and like to pray for people we meet. Is there something we can pray for?"

She said, "What?" After removing her headset, she said, "I'm deaf in my left ear and couldn't hear you." That's because the headset was covering her good ear. She said she started losing hearing in that ear at age three. That immediately told my friend what to pray for.

He asked, "Would it offend you if I prayed for your left ear to hear again?" She didn't answer; she just stuck both hands out the window to hold his hands during the prayer! That took him by surprise, but he was in the Bible belt, so *maybe that's normal here*, he thought.

Friends, it was like she was waiting for someone to pray for her ear! So he did what any of us should do: he thanked God for her by name (Erica), he directed the spirit of deafness to leave her left ear in the name of Jesus, and then he spoke affirming words of life to her. She thanked him and said what "a good day" it was.

Now, according to him, she didn't get her hearing back instantly, but he believes she will because three people were in agreement over that, and we read that Jesus restored hearing to the deaf (in both ears) more than once.

As my friend and his son were driving away from Wendy's, what just happened hit him so suddenly he stopped the car. It dawned on him there had been no real danger that he would not get his dental appliance back at all! Losing it (where he did), finding it (when he did), and being hungry (when he was) were all orchestrated by God to let that Wendy's gal know that He loves her and cares about her victory over deafness. God hadn't forgotten her and sent a messenger (all the way from a small town in Washington to a medium town in Georgia) to let her know so!

That's the God we serve. Can you see how exciting life can be when you are Spirit-led and are obedient to that leading? He takes us through a struggle (often of our own doing), and He blesses a complete stranger (through us) as the reward for the struggle that we went through. What a faith builder!

In my case, I thought I was going back to Dallas to *get my luggage*. In God's mind that was not the main thing. It was the ripple effect of *blessing the claims gal*. My buddy thought, in his mind, the mission was to *get his denture back*. But no, it wasn't. It was to *bless the Wendy's worker*. Getting the teeth back was a ripple effect, an earthly means to a heavenly end.

I DARE YOU to be open to living the way of life God has for you. That's being open to what His will is for you today. Maybe it's to read this book! Maybe it's to set this book aside and read God's Word. I don't know. Like for my buddy and me, what may start out as a normal or routine thing in life can yield unexpected results. Not unexpected to God. Unexpected to us!

> "What other people label or might try
> to call failure, I have learned is just God's
> way of pointing you in a new direction."
> **- Oprah Winfrey**

*For it is God who works in you to will and
to act in order to fulfill his good purpose.*
- Philippians 2:13

May you walk in a manner worthy of your calling.

REMINDER: We are not victims of our circumstances; children are. We, as adults, are victims of our choices. *Choose wisely. Choose Holy Spirit.*

4

AND MY GOD IS . . .

BEFORE WE BEGIN to go too far down the road of living life under the influence of the Holy Spirit, let's answer a critical, all-important question: *Who is your God?* Simultaneously: *What is your god?*

Suppose you are given this definition of your god:

Your god is who or what you first think of when you wake up each day and the last person, place, or thing you think of when you go to bed.

Now, with that as our definition on the table, ask yourself: Who or what is my god?

This is a time to be real and honest with ourselves. I know we're starting out with some heavy stuff, but this is no time for a fluffy chapter. Scripture doesn't merely suggest that people examine themselves in **1 Corinthians 11**. It's a *need to* thing.

Some saints do it every day, others just before taking Communion, still others not at all! The point is if we didn't need to examine ourselves, God wouldn't have told us to, right? So what does "examine yourself" look like? It's not what we see in the mirror on the wall. It's what we see in the intents of our heart and mind.

Below is a sample list of first waking-up thoughts and an interpretation (read: *my* interpretation) of who your your god is, based on that thought.

I think of:	My god may be:
Coffee	Self (via coffee)
Horoscope	Self (via divination)
Breath (smell)	Self
Bodily functions (gotta go)	Self
Spouse	Self (via spouse)
Non-spouse	Self (again)
How tired I am	Self
The kids	Self (via the kids)
Pet(s)	Self (via pets)
Aches/pains	Self
The news	Self
Music/bands	Self (via music)
Internet/computer	Self
Work	Self (via work)
Hobbies	Self
The neighbors	Self (via pride)

Can we agree there is a pattern here? Ninety-nine percent of people begin each and every day by *think-*

ing of themselves. (I know I have.) But is that the way it's meant to be for the believer? How is that any different from an unbeliever? *Nada!* No different.

Mike, who cares what I think about as I wake up? That's a good question. Here is the answer from God's word: "For where your treasure is, there your heart will be also." **(Matthew 6)** Takeaway: treasure = heart.

Now, is it fair to assume that what we treasure the most is what we think about the most? *Of course!* The treasure has an impact on our thoughts throughout the day: first thing, last thing, and anywhere in between.

Do we have any examples in Scripture? **Daniel 1** tells us that "Daniel purposed in his heart that he would not defile himself" (of the worldly things available to him). (NKJV) He treasured being a holy young man in a pagan society. **Daniel 6** reveals that Daniel got on his knees three times a day to pray and give thanks to God morning, noon, and night. (That's not to imply there weren't other prayers throughout the day where he couldn't kneel.)

In **Psalm 63** King David says to God: "When I remember You on my bed, I meditate on You in the night watches." (NKJV) Since they didn't have clocks on the wall in those days, a crier (or watchman) would be tasked with announcing each new hour as it came to the people in the city or village. That tells us that if the watchman's pronouncement woke David up, he would make good use of the interruption to meditate on the Lord (his treasure).

So David thought about God not only while going to bed but also all through the night! **Psalm 92** says: "It is good to give thanks to the LORD, and to sing praises to Your name, O Most High; To declare Your lovingkindness in the morning, and Your faithfulness every night." (NKJV) These verses reveal an intentionality based on the heart.

As the words *mercy* and *truth* are knit together throughout Scripture, so are the words *heart* and *mind*:

> Test me, LORD, and try me, examine my
> heart and my mind. (**Psalm 26**)

> I the LORD search the heart and examine
> the mind, to reward each person according
> to their conduct, and according to what
> their deeds deserve. (**Jeremiah 17**)

So the heart is referenced as the area where our emotions and intentions reside. The mind is where our will and actions spring forth.

In every murder trial in the country, the prosecutor has to prove two things:

1. that the defendant had a depraved heart (that is, he or she was numb to the sanctity of another human's life) and

2. what was going on inside the murderer's mind. The legal Latin term is *mens rea*, (MENZ RAY-ah), but we would simply say *motive* (the thought behind the action).

Now we are certain that the judge or jury will be trying to discern the defendant's heart and mind before and during the crime. The *what* of the case deals with the heart. The *how* deals with the means of death, but the *why* deals with the mind of the perpetrator (what was in his or her head at the time).

[Side note: our hearts can think and our minds can feel according to **Proverbs 23:7a** and **Isaiah 26:3**. It is over my pay grade to begin to explain that.]

In modern Christian life, we may seek out books to learn *how to* have a godly life. Oddly enough, God doesn't care about the *how*; He cares about your heart (the *what*) and your mind (the *why*). It's the *why* behind the *what* that is dominant yet so ignored today.

Do you want a successful Christian life? I've got news for you: *that's not important.* That's because you being a successful Christian is not on God's radar. Plus, we can't even judge what a successful Christian is due to the inherent weaknesses of our humanity, so we're ill-equipped to know when we have arrived!

Even the apostle Paul admitted this in **Philippians 3**: "Not that I have already obtained all this or have already arrived at my goal, but I press on to possess that perfection for which Christ Jesus first possessed me."

No, God doesn't want us to be *successful*; He wants us to be *fruitful* in His kingdom, "that you may live a life worthy of the Lord and please him in every way: bearing fruit in every good work, growing in the knowledge of God." **(Colossians 1)**

Know this: the path to fruitfulness is *faithfulness*, and the only path to faithfulness is the *working of the Holy Spirit* in your life and mine. So this book is devoted to this paradigm:

Holy Spirit ==> Faithfulness ==> Fruitfulness

We cannot fail if we stick to God's scriptural model of faithful availability.

Notice, I didn't say *faithful performance*. Why? Because it's not about performance. It's about abiding in Christ, His Spirit abiding in you, and your availability to seek and do God's will. Every day. *But what if I am not available to God on a given day, and I don't seek His will for my life that day? What then?*

Well, rather than say that you screwed up and deserve to get punished, I would say that you probably missed out on what you could have experienced in God. The loss is temporal, not eternal. You simply did *without* when you could have done *with*. "With God nothing will be impossible." (**Luke 1**, NKJV)

If this sounds like lots of work, then we are thinking in our human mind and missing the point. Jesus said: "My yoke is *easy* and my burden is *light*." (**Matthew 11**, emphasis added.) When our life is hard, we know that we are not truly giving our burden to Jesus and receiving His (light) burden back to us. The enemy wants it that way because it's the only way believers live defeated lives. *Why is Jesus's burden light?* Because He has won both His victory and our victory!

Are you tired of living a defeated life? One that you can't fix? Then go all-in with what Jesus offers: your burden for His, and His Holy Spirit for your human spirit. "This I say . . . Walk by the Spirit and [you] shall not fulfill the lust of the flesh." (**Galatians 5**, KJV) In the next chapter we'll take a deep dive into what walking in the Spirit looks like. Find **Romans 8** to have on hand when you read it.

I DARE YOU to lean on the Spirit of God to bring you to a depth of faithfulness that will result in fruitfulness for His kingdom.

"Being faithful in the smallest things is the way to gain, maintain, and demonstrate the strength needed to accomplish something great."
– Alex Harris

He who is faithful in what is least is faithful also in much.
– Luke 16:10 (NKJV)

May you stop bearing your burdens over and over again, expecting a different result. Give your burdens to Jesus. He alone is your burden bearer. Be yoked to Him.

REMINDER: We are not victims of our circumstances; children are. We, as adults, are victims of our choices. *Choose wisely. Choose Holy Spirit.*

5

TAKE A WALK ON THE WILD SIDE

LIFE IS LIKE crossing a high canyon on a single rope with a guide rope above your head. Step by measured step, you precariously tread through life and all its challenges: youth, school, sports, relationships, marriage, health issues, employment, habits, hobbies, responsibilities, and so on.

The Holy Spirit is like a guide rope above. The Spirit is not the foundation (what you're walking on) but the guide (or Helper) to keep you on the foundation. Yeah, it may be possible to cross over the canyon without a guide rope, but so much more dangerous, stressful, and prone to destruction. The key is to remember that the guide rope is there—all the way! As believers, we know the Holy Spirit is always there for us. Remember that, and employ the guide rope; walk by the Spirit of God.

OK, Mike, sounds good, but . . . that is not how I live. To be honest, I call all the shots in my day-to-day life, my crossing of life's canyon. How do I fit the Holy Spirit into my day-to-day?

The concept of fitting the Holy Spirit into our day is pretty *me-focused*, right? To get it right, we don't fit the Spirit in; instead, we just want to *fit in with* the Spirit of God. We want to sound like, act like, and view others like . . . the Holy Spirit.

Why do you want to be Spirit led? What are your expectations or inhibitions? What's the worst that can happen if we live by the Spirit? Yes, our rope will be rocked from time to time, but as long as we're stepping in God's direction, using His Helper, we'll come out ahead.

We don't live just to be *anti-Satan*. We live also to please God as we experience His goodness and His provision of "everything we need for a godly life." (**2 Peter 1**) That is a promise. Included in His promise and provision for believers is the *resurrection power* of Jesus. He paid for it all!

But it doesn't stop there. We are to consume Him on such a deep, spiritual basis that it affects our spirit, soul, and body:

> **Romans 8:** The mind governed by the
> flesh is death, but the mind governed
> by the Spirit is life and peace. The mind

governed by the flesh is hostile to God;
it does not submit to God's law, nor can it
do so.

1 Corinthians 2: The [natural] person
without the Spirit does not accept the
things that come from the Spirit of God
but considers them foolishness, and
cannot understand them because they
are discerned only through the Spirit.

By these two verses we come to know that a world-ly, carnal human (by nature) is clueless to grasping things at the spirit level. Accordingly, a person living in a two-dimensional world cannot see, know, or experience anything in a third dimension.

There are far too many professing Christians living in a two-dimensional world (Father and Son only). You saw more details of this in the chapter "Father, Son, and. . . ." As a consequence, they miss the glorious and fulfilling dimension of the Holy Spirit.

That is a big reason modern churches are so weak and powerless. They pay homage to a two-dimensional Trinity, the Father and the Son, or to a false three-dimen-sional Trinity of the Father, Son, and Holy *Bible*. The only real third dimension of the Trinity is the Holy Spirit! Our life in God must consist of all parts to be wholly His and holy His!

Ever plant a seed potato? The best way is not to plant only the eye of a potato (you know, the nubby sprout that pops out after being in the pantry too long) but to put the whole potato in the ground. *Why?* Because the new potato shoots will feed on the decomposed potato that is all around it. That is, the new life feeds on its source.

Jesus is the source of our life, and we need to feed on Him. If we don't, we either won't make it, or at best, our growth will be stunted because we'll be grossly undernourished. As our source, He gives His children the Holy Spirit to keep us fed once we've sprouted.

*Do you still have **Romans 8** handy?* It is a wonderful, God-inspired guidebook to life in the Spirit. Please read it for yourself, but here is my take on **verses 1-5**:

1: We are no longer under condemnation (in Jesus). Meaning you're not guilty! *So why do you feel guilty?* If there is no guilt, there's no punishment for that guilt! Remember, *guilt is not a feeling; it is a state of being.* For some reason, believers (who are declared *not guilty*) feel guilty and non-believers (who are declared *guilty*) don't feel guilty. *Does that make sense?*

2: Under the new law of the Spirit of life, we are free (in Jesus) from the old law. There are no valid indictments against us in the old law. What *was there* has been paid in full by our Savior.

3: God (in Jesus) condemned sin in the flesh.

4: We walk in the Spirit and not in the flesh (our old way of living). As Jesus revealed, He does not say or do anything "but what He sees the Father do." (**John 5**, NKJV) We are to do and say what we see and hear by the Spirit.

5: All who live according to the Spirit set their minds on the *things of the Spirit.*

[Side Note: Does Scripture explain what the "things of the Spirit" are? Of course! First, we look to **Galatians 5** to see the fruit (or results) of the things of the Spirit: "love, joy, peace, forbearance, kindness, goodness, faithfulness, gentleness and self-control."]

So setting our mind on the Spirit is a mindset. For most of us, that requires a shift in our thinking. If we don't shift, we are prone to negative, sinful thoughts. Remember, *shift* happens.

A pastor in Georgia, Dr. Henry Wright, was known for his southern way of describing those negative thoughts we tend to have as "stinking thinking." It's easy enough to recognize such thoughts. We are commanded (and deputized) to arrest those thoughts and take them captive. (**2 Corinthians 10**) Basically, we are to run them out of town, out of our mind.

We needn't force our mind on the Spirit to get the Spirit. Rather, in having the Spirit, it is second nature to set our mental clocks accordingly. That looks like **Galatians 5** (ESV): "And those who belong to Christ Jesus have crucified the flesh with its passions and desires. [That would include our addictions, friends.] If we live by the Spirit, let us also keep in step with the Spirit."

Don't miss the word *if*. It validates that professing to belong to Jesus does not automatically cause us to live by the Spirit. It is a *purposed lifestyle*, not merely a club membership. It implies we can get *out of* step when our mind gets off Christ.

What happens when we get out of step? Lose our way? Feel left behind? We pray (even if we don't feel like praying). One young lady was struggling in her prayer life. She had lost the "want to," and it was becoming a "have to" ritual each day. She really enjoys music and found that if she sang a hymn or two, her soul was in the right mode to begin her prayers. That's insightfully adjusting to our needs, while praising the Lord.

We don't live a life of self-control (something we may have rarely experienced in the past) without intentionality and obedience to God's Word on our part. When we *think* the right things, it becomes natural to *do* right things.

For that, we look to **Philippians 4** for those right things:

whatever is true,

whatever is noble,

whatever is right,

whatever is pure,

whatever is lovely,

whatever is admirable—

if anything is excellent [in virtue] or praiseworthy— think about such things.

Now, the picture comes into more focus! We think and meditate on truth, honor, justice, purity, loveliness, good words (reports), and not only those but also anything virtuous and praiseworthy. *All these adjectives seem to point us to God's holy Word, don't they?*

When we track with these things, our thoughts lead to a heart-change of holiness and living under the influence of the Holy Spirit. We get a new GPS (godly positioning system). Our commitment to follow that GPS (fueled by faith *in* God and obedience *to* God) is the by-product of having the fruit of the Spirit!

Do we have to make it more complicated than that? *No way!* It's the enemy of our souls that constantly wants to complicate things and make a life of obedience seem altogether unreachable (and not worth the effort). Don't let that lie stick on you! He's deceiving us with the same intent as he deceived Eve and Adam.

To observe Satan's playbook, let's look at the *antonyms* of the list in **Philippians 4**. The enemy would have us contemplate whatever is:

false or misleading,

beneath honor,

unjust/defrauding,

impure/smarmy/scandalous,

unpleasant and disagreeable,

damnable and disgusting—

if there's anything filthy, raunchy, defrauding to men, women, and (especially) children, worthy of all condemnation—think about those things.

See? That is how the devil rolls (operates). He doesn't mind messing with our minds so we don't operate with the mind of Christ (which is a promise in **1 Corinthians 2** to believers in Jesus).

When we walk in the Spirit, we (daily) crucify the influence of Satan in our day-to-day lives because he no longer has a badge; he does not call the shots. We owe no more response to an encounter with him than resisting him in Jesus's name. **James 4** assures us of a good outcome to that resistance.

I DARE YOU to cross the rope of your life by hanging onto the Guide Rope above that Jesus promised us.

> "The Word makes known what we alone know about ourselves—and often what we do not yet know about ourselves. Scripture plunges deep into the unseen places of the human spirit and judges the private matters of the heart. Only the razor-sharp Word of God can do this."
> **– Steven J. Lawson**

> *Take the helmet of salvation and the sword of the Spirit, which is the word of God. And pray in the Spirit on all occasions with all kinds of prayers and requests. With this in mind, be alert and always keep on praying for all the Lord's people.*
> **– Ephesians 6:17-18**

May you see what the Spirit sees (in people and situations), say what the Spirit would say, and do what the Spirit would do.

REMINDER: We are not victims of our circumstances; children are. We, as adults, are victims of our choices. *Choose wisely. Choose Holy Spirit.*

6

WE ARE ALL TRANS

THAT IS A TRUE STATEMENT of fact. If it wasn't, it wouldn't be in this book.

OK, Mike, where are you going with this?

Well, think about it for a minute. If I asked you if you have ever *sinned*, would you say yes? (I would.) I guess that makes us sinners, right? If I asked you if you have ever been involved in *iniquity*, would you also say yes? (I would too.) That makes us human.

There's another thing that God said He forgave in **Numbers 14**. Would you say yes to ever committing a *transgression*? (#Metoo!) I guess that makes us trans-gressors.

Wait a minute! We're "trans" because we're trans-gressors? *Duh!* That's what I mean when I say we are all trans. But what does the term really mean? The dictionary says *transgressor* is a noun that is defined as *someone who transgresses; violating a law, or command, or going beyond a boundary or limit*. In other words, a trans is someone who crosses the line. That means Adam and Eve were trans because they crossed a limit that God had made known to them. (*Do not eat of this tree.*)

Now we can get practical. Have I ever pushed over a limit that was communicated to me? Yep, and so have you! Let's talk about highway speed limits. *Ever gone above the speed limit? Maybe way above?* It doesn't matter how much over. Either way, you *trans*gressed a legal limit.

For years, a friend of mine would milk his Jersey cow at his home in one state and supply some raw milk to people at his church in another state. It just seemed natural to do that. But he later found out that it's (like) a felony to distribute raw milk interstate.

Whether he knew it was illegal or not, he definitely transgressed that federal law. He was a transgressor by definition.

Sin, the overarching term, is defined in Scripture multiple ways. In **James 4** it says: "If anyone, then, knows the good they ought to do and doesn't do it, it is sin for them." That's the sin of *omission*. In other words, I could have done the right thing, but I chose not to do it.

Every offense of the Ten Commandments is a sin of *commission* (telling a lie, stealing something, using the Lord's name crassly, etc.). Elsewhere, **Romans 14** says that "everything that does not come from faith is sin."

That's a pretty high bar. In general, we have defined sin as *missing the mark*. Other terms we use are coming up short, blowing it, messing up, screwing up, and *my bad!*

Iniquity is not just sin but also *the propensity* towards sin. Scripture suggests that it can be passed down from generation to generation. We look to **Exodus 20**: "For I, the LORD your God, am a jealous God, visiting the iniquity of the fathers to the children to the third and fourth generations of those who hate Me." (NKJV) What's the root iniquity? *Hating God.*

I know of families that had a propensity towards alcoholism, others towards gluttony or smoking. Here is a wise proverb, spoken by a former youth leader in Chicago: *What parents excuse in moderation, their children will excuse in excess.* That means their filter between *enough* and *no I want more* is not as effective as your knowing when to stop (or limit) that activity, like gambling. They learn from you, how to hold 'em but haven't learned when to fold 'em—or to, perhaps, stay away from addictive things altogether.

Now, we cannot add to Holy Scripture by saying things are in there that God did not say or ascribe actions to God that He did not do. For example, we cannot tell someone the Word says that all left-handed people are the elect of God. Clearly, He never said that. True, left-handed people are not *excluded* from being God's people, but they surely do not comprise the whole.

That said, I don't believe it is unscriptural to apply what we know from His Word to alternative situations, meaning if we set the beginning of **John 8** to the present, it might be paraphrased as follows:

> The teachers of the Law and Pharisees brought a man who looks (very much) like a woman to Jesus. "Rabbi, this man has been caught looking like, dressing like, talking like, and smelling like a woman. You can see that for Yourself. We understand the Law commands us to stone such a person, but what do You say?"
>
> Jesus was sitting (bent over) writing on the ground with His finger. After they continued to nag Him, He stood up and said, "Let anyone of you who is without sin cast the first stone."
>
> Upon hearing Him, and being pierced in their own conscience, they went out one by one, beginning with the oldest, till all had left.
>
> Jesus looked at the guy (in drag) and said, "Son of Abraham, where are your accusers? Has no one condemned you?"

The man replied, "No one, Lord." Jesus said unto him, "Neither do I condemn you, friend. Now that you've met Me, you have the grace to leave your life of sin."

Whether you read the paraphrase (above) or the actual account in **John 8:3-11** (a real woman, caught in real adultery with a real man), our takeaway is at least this: there *was* a man there who was without sin (when the accusers came), and He had every right to throw the first stone . . . but He didn't! In fact, Jesus did the opposite by saying, "I do not condemn you."

Folks, we are all that woman—guilty as sin. We are all trans! And Jesus is telling us the same thing: *I do not condemn you, Mike. I have given you (as a believer in Me) victory over sin. That's our victory! Your victory and Mine! I settled the account and wrote you a check. You just get to believe and cash it as you abide in Me.*

His desire is for us to be like Him: loving and compassionate enough to give up His right (and only His right) to cast the first stone and actually express concern for that person who messed up, who failed, who broke the rules, who stabbed you in the back, who insulted you, who cost you money.

That's how Jesus wants us to be with all people who are trans. Yes, Jesus loves a trans person unconditionally, just as He loved that adulterous woman unconditionally, but real love doesn't accommodate sin in others.

Real love demonstrates (with power and compassion) how to go from being a victim of sin to being a victor over sin! You can't have a foot in both camps. The Word says in **John 8**: *"So if the Son sets you free, you will be free indeed."* That's a freedom you and I can take to the bank!

But Mike, I thought unconditional love means never having to say "I'm sorry" for anything I've done. At least, that was the theme in the movie Love Story.

I know, but this is real life.

You know what happens when I honestly say to you "I'm sorry"? It means I'm humbling myself *in the moment.* I'm caring for you more than myself—to the point of humility. That's real love.

Jesus humbled Himself to leave Heaven and come to planet Earth as a man. Then, as a man, He lived a humble life for three years (homeless, itinerant) and died the most humiliating death. He did all that for *trans*, like you and me.

Besides, if you never hear me say, "I'm sorry," I'll never get to hear you say, "I forgive you, Mike." It takes real love to forgive, and it takes real humility to lovingly ask for forgiveness.

My concluding thought is that we are all born trans-gressors and that when we yield to Christ, we become trans-formed. Either way, we are trans.

I DARE YOU to understand that being led by the Holy Spirit will result in the most fruitful life that we can't even imagine. Why? Because we're not trying to do it by ourselves. Let's live our lives as though "our sins and our lawless deeds" will be "remember[ed] no more," and move on to maturity *in* God and peace *with* God. (**Hebrews 8** NKJV)

> "If you want to be led by the Spirit of God, then devote yourself to the Word of God."
> **– J. D. Greear**

> *Do not conform to the pattern of this world, but be transformed by the renewing of your mind. Then you will be able to test and approve what God's will is—His good, pleasing and perfect will.*
> **– Romans 12:2**

May you live as though there are no burdens weighing you down because the only burdens you will find are the ones you didn't put on Christ.

REMINDER: We are not victims of our circumstances; children are. We, as adults, are victims of our choices. *Choose wisely. Choose Holy Spirit.*

PICK YOUR PREACHER

YOU MAY HAVE SUNG THE classic children's Sunday school song that goes:

> *Oh, be careful little ears what you hear.*
> *Oh, be careful little ears what you hear.*
> There's a Father up above
> And He's looking down in love.
> So be careful little ears what you hear.

Those words are just as relevant to adults as they are to children. In fact, I would say *more so* because adults live with way more self-autonomy than toddlers. We can (largely) dictate what we listen to.

From the moment we're born, our ears take in an astonishing amount of sounds (even before birth, actually). At first hospital sounds, parents, and nurses' voices. When baby is brought home, then all sorts of voices: TV shows, movies, and lyrics from rock songs, country, R&B,

rap, hip hop, elevator music, maybe even Christ-honoring songs.

Babies hear laughter, crying, singing, moaning (or maybe snoring), dogs barking, birds twittering, leaves rustling, alarms going off, vacuums running. The point is our ears are full-time receivers of sounds.

Some voices are good for us to hear. Those voices are soothing, instructive, and come from people who love and care about us. Other voices are irritating, agitating, hurtful, confusing, and come from people who love and care only for themselves and their agenda.

With our ears we strain to hear a whisper, and we also cover them to protect us from very loud noises (like fireworks) or very loud yelling (like an argument). Good stewardship of our ears will help them last longer. But more importantly, good stewardship keeps our ears from taking in lies of the enemy. Imagine if Eve had taken better care of her ears in the Garden.

There are so many voices in the world that are competing for our attention. *Once they have our attention, they can wield influence and control.* Parents have influence. Friends have influence. Teachers have influence. The press has influence. Celebrities have influence. Politicians have influence. Heck, Dr. Phil and Oprah have influence.

What do they call people on social media with a gagillion followers? Influencers! *Hello?* The bottom line isn't whether there are enough influencers out there. The bottom line is *whom do we subscribe to?* To whom do we give the keys to our eyes and our ears to let the influencers have their way?

There is a meme that says, *To follow God, you must unfollow the world.* That (about) sums up this chapter. Hose it down any way you want, but we subscribe to (or follow) those we admire. Period. End of story. Whether you follow Candace Owens or Stacey Abrams, Kanye West or Joe Rogan, it still comes down to you admiring them because what they say resonates with you.

The voices we hear are more important than we know. **Romans 10** says, "Everyone who calls on the name of the Lord will be saved." (Amen!) But what follows is a logic trail: "How, then, can they call on the One they have not believed in? And how can they believe in the One they have not heard? And how can they hear without someone preaching to them?"

In all phases in life, we are being preached at. I can tell you, firsthand, that when I work with fitness trainers at the gym, they are constantly preaching fitness to me. Soccer coaches preach soccer. That goes for football, baseball, basketball, volleyball, track, and swimming coaches too. Dance instructors preach ballet. Science instructors preach evolutionism (whether they believe it or not). Doctors preach diet and exercise. Dentists preach hygiene. At my day job, I preach wealth management and proactive investing.

It all gets back to my point on voices. *We don't have to be sitting in a pew to be preached at.* In fact, for most of us, that is the least amount of preaching we take in any given week. *What?* Maybe thirty minutes to an hour? I can easily spend two hours at my fitness center. That's double the preaching I hear in church in a week!

Friends, we have to be intentional about whom we are listening to and why we are listening to them. Put another way, why are we not listening to God more? *Why aren't the sheep hearing the Shepherd?*

The two-word answer is Holy Spirit. If we're not taking care to desire the Holy Spirit to tune our receivers to the things of the Lord, there are plenty of preachers (of distractions) out there. Even if we've had a Holy Spirit indwelling experience, we must (daily) yield our personal spirit (and will) to the Holy Spirit. It sounds counterintuitive, but daily surrendering is the first step to daily victory!

We'll close out this chapter with the testimony of a Christian attorney named David Gibbs Jr. (DG). (FYI, forty years ago, he founded Christian Law Association, CLA, which is like an ACLU for pastors and homeschoolers around the country.) Years ago, he was on CLA business among the Aleutian Islands in Alaska and was ready to head home (to Ohio) via Anchorage.

He and his associate were about to fly out commercially when a pastor said he could save them some money. It turns out he was a private pilot and he'd flown his plane there and was flying back to Anchorage anyway. Against David's better judgment, he agreed to fly with the pastor instead because he was so insistent.

The next day, they boarded the small plane after the pilot did his exterior inspections. They taxied out to the runway while David was praying for the pilot and the plane that was carrying the three men. They effortlessly lifted off the runway, and David was thankful for such a smooth ascent.

After about four minutes, they ascended into their designated flight elevation, which put them into an endless cloud bank. At that point, the pastor/pilot turned to Mr. Gibbs and chose *that* moment to confess that he cannot fly in clouds because they make him pass out! As David was asking if he heard him right, the man's eyes rolled back into his head and he was out cold!

David shook him vigorously and said, "You've got to wake up." Not happening. *Lights out.* Nobody home. *Bye, bye.* The associate asked Mr. Gibbs, "We're dead, aren't we? What are we going to do?" His boss handed him the radio microphone and told him to try to get some help.

The associate made awkward, panicked, efforts to communicate. Eventually, a freight pilot (going from Anchorage to Tokyo) picked up the signal and asked what was wrong. They told him they lost their pilot and that no one can fly the plane. The freighter pilot immediately recognized the seriousness of the situation and reached out to Anchorage Emergency (AE) to make radar and audio contact with them.

Thank God for autopilot, which kept the men both on course and at elevation. AE radioed the stranded passengers. From here on, you'll read the words they spoke to each other:

> AE "We understand you have a passed-out pilot and none of you can fly the plane."
> DG "That's right."

David interjects (to us), *"I'll never forget what the man in Anchorage said."*

> AE "My job is to get you home safe. That's my job. But here's the deal. If you want me to get you home safe, you gotta promise me you will obey my voice. You can't see me, but I can see you. If you're not going to obey my voice, you're gonna die."

David interjects: *"When you can't see anything, you've no idea how disoriented you become."*

AE "Now hear me clear. You're four minutes from a mountain. You're going to crash in that mountain and die . . . so follow my voice."

David interjects: *"I never questioned [this man's role] because I understood that without his voice I had NOTHING! Do you understand? Without God's voice you have nothing!"*

The man got them turned to safety and let them know he had frozen all the air traffic between them and the airport. He also said it would take an hour and a half to get to Anchorage.

AE "There's a lot of weather between you and Anchorage. You're in for a rough ride. I want you to hear me. I don't want you to look at what's going on outside. I don't want you to pay attention to the storm—just my voice. If you start watching the storm, you will die. But I'll take you through it."

David interjects: *"Because they cleared all the traffic, several pilots (those nighttime 747 freighters) started talking to us. They said, 'We're praying for you, men. You're gonna make it! Listen to the voice. That's the key. Trust the voice.'"*

David asks us, *"Do you realize your head is full of voices? Everyone wants to talk to you, and they want to be the controlling voice. God says, 'I want you to be a living sacrifice. I want you to put yourself on the altar and let My voice be your voice.'*

"Finally, we got through the worst of the weather and the voice came back."

AE "Now, I'm gonna line you up. I'm gonna bring you in, right down the runway. At the foot of the runway are some lights, and they're in the form of a cross. Don't you forget this: the cross is the way home."

David interjects: *"Finally, he's bringing us down. We still can't see anything as he's telling us to stay with him [stay the course]. The Bible says, 'My sheep hear My voice and they follow Me.' Soon, a couple hundred feet off the ground, we saw the cross and I landed the plane. In fact, we landed [touched down] seven times! Soon, we came to a stop, and the pilot woke up.*

AE "Thanks for listening. I watch 'em crash and burn all the time because they won't follow my voice. They don't understand I am the one who can see them, even though they can't see me. They get the voices in their head and they self-destruct. Thanks for listening to my voice."

Next, the emergency folks put them in a motel room for the night. Hours later, there was a knock on the door. David opened it and saw a man standing there.

"Hello, David."

"You're the one!" David said, recognizing the voice. "You're the one who got me home."

"I am," said the AE guy, smiling.

David interjects to us once more: *"Do you understand that one day, you're going to stand before Jesus and say, 'You're the voice? You're the voice that brought me home?'"*

David Gibbs Jr. reminds us that if we're not listening to the Holy Spirit, our heads will be full of other voices. And we wonder why our marriages are fractured and our kids crash and burn. All the while, *Holy Spirit is saying: I'm the voice. I will take you home.*

Remember the autopilot? No question that it kept them from spiraling down to Earth, but it is not reliable for every situation. In four minutes, it would have flown them into the side of a mountain. That score is easy to predict: Mountain – 1, Plane – 0. Three lives would have been lost on impact. We cannot risk our eternal lives to autopilot, whatever your autopilot is: religion, good works, donations, and so on.

Mr. Gibbs makes it plain that if we are not hearing God's voice for our decisions and plans, we are listening to other voices. We haven't yet *unfollowed* the world, the flesh, and the devil, then those voices subtly direct our thoughts away from God and onto others or ourselves. We listen to them, we get disoriented, we get lost in the storm of life. But God is always there to take us through. All we have to do is hear His voice and obey.

I DARE YOU to tune out the world's voices and listen to the Holy Spirit's voice each and every day.

> "There will be no peace in any soul until it is willing to obey the voice of God."
> **– Dwight L. Moody**

> *I stand at the door and knock. If anyone hears my voice and opens the door, I will come in and eat with that person, and they with me.*
> **– Revelation 3:20**

May you choose your preachers wisely.

REMINDER: We are not victims of our circumstances; children are. We, as adults, are victims of our choices. *Choose wisely. Choose Holy Spirit.*

Part 11

TEST THE QUALITY/BRAND

SECRET AGENT MAN

THE SECRET OF GOD IS Christ in you, the hope of glory. (**Colossians 1**) It's a secret. He's telling us: *I want you to partake of what I've done as far as the covenant is, and you don't do anything* **at all**. *You didn't do anything but enter into the covenant with Me and the Father and the Spirit. We did it all.* You get to enter. That's the secret. Those are the people that fear God, who say, "I want to enter into the New (Gospel) Covenant."

Why do I refer to the first thirty-nine books of God's Word as the First Covenant? Because the use of the word *old* has the connotation that it is not relevant anymore. *Nothing could be further from the truth!* That precious body of Scriptures was relevant to Jesus, so they'd better be relevant to us. I call the remaining twenty-seven books the New Covenant, but it would be more accurate to say "the Last Covenant" or "Gospel Covenant."

If that was our understanding, then Jesus saying (in **Revelation 1**) that He is "the Alpha and the Omega, the Beginning and the End" (NKJV) takes on a deeper meaning. Jesus is the First (Covenant) AND the Last (Covenant). His holiness, love, and sacrifice are evident in both! We can't treat them like oil and water. But many people and churches do—to their own detriment.

Another term for *secret* is mystery. Mystery almost implies that something can't be known or solved, OR conversely, if it can be known or solved, it is only for a select few. For ages, the coming of Christ was a mystery. In fact, it was such a mystery that God's people got it all wrong! In the flesh, the Hebrews (who were under Roman tribute when Jesus was thirty) reasoned that the Messiah would swoop in as a conqueror and send the Romans fleeing back to Italy.

It was not to be. They were told that *The One* would be born in Bethlehem. (**Micah 5**) They were told He would be born of a virgin. (**Isaiah 7**) They were told that Elijah would come before Him. (**Malachi 4**) They were told He would make a new covenant. (**Jeremiah 31**) They were told He would be called "God's Son." (**Psalm 2**) They were told His body would not see decay and He would ascend into Heaven. (**Psalm 16**) They were told He would be a prophet similar to Moses. (**Deuteronomy 18**) They were told He would be hated without a cause and false witnesses would rise up against Him. (**Psalm 35**) They were told He would delight to do God's will. (**Psalm 40**) They were told He would be betrayed for thirty pieces of silver. (**Psalm 41** and **Zechariah 11**) They were told He would inherit an eternal throne. (**Psalm 45** and **89**) They were told He would speak in parables. (**Psalm 78**) They were told He would be a Priest according to the Order of Melchizedek. (**Psalm 110**) They were told He would be known as the Son of Man, to whom God had given everlasting dominion and glory and a kingdom that all nations and peoples should serve Him. (**Daniel 7**) They were told that the stone which the builders [Jews] rejected would become the chief cornerstone. (**Psalm 118**) They were told He would ride into Jerusalem on a donkey. (**Zechariah 9**) They were told He would pray for His adversaries. (**Psalm 109**) They were told that not one bone of His would be broken. (**Psalm 34**) They were told that His face would be beaten beyond recognition. (**Isaiah 53** and **Zechariah 12**) They were told that His hands and feet would be pierced, that He would thirst, and that men would remove His garments and cast lots (gamble) for them. Also, that those around would say, "He trusted on the Lord. Let Him deliver Him, seeing He delights in Him." And that He, Himself, would say: "My God, my God, why have you forsaken me?" (**Psalm 22**) They were told He would ascend into Heaven. (**Psalm 68**). They were told He would be seated in Heaven at the right hand of the Father. (**Psalm 110**) They were told He would be the Prince of Peace. (**Isaiah 9**) They were told He is the Sun of Righteousness with healing in His wings. (**Malachi 4**)

With all these First Covenant prophecies (and many more), the nation of Israel still could not recognize the Messiah (Melekh Mashiach) because He didn't fit their mold (of a conquering Messiah, not a humble, suffering Messiah). *How could this be?* Why didn't they rejoice in the mystery being unveiled before their very eyes? The answer is also in prophecy.

Isaiah 6 says: "Make the heart of the [Hebrew] people calloused; make their ears dull and close their eyes. Otherwise they might see with their eyes, hear with their ears, understand with their hearts, and turn and be healed." Turn from what? From reliance on the works of the Law for salvation, from their wicked ways, and from their false concept of the Messiah.

Paul reveals a mystery in **Romans 11** that out of God's mercy, He blinded the eyes of the Jews in order to open salvation up to the Gentiles and grafted them into the Vine of salvation. *Thank God!* We are indebted to the Jews for their role in that. Without them, there would be no Christianity.

But, Mike, if that was true then, it may surely be true now. Why bother reaching out to those who won't listen or see?

I get that.

Our job, as Spirit-led (and Spirit-filled) secret agents is to share that Holy secret with everyone we can! But modern Christianity looks more and more like a secret society to those on the outside: with titles and customs and songs and rituals and closed membership. *That is not our lane.* We are to be open to share the Good News with anybody the Lord brings our way.

We know we have lost our badge when we tell people they need to talk to a pastor or priest. No, friends, if you have God's Word, you are equipped and mandated to use it to bless others and lead them to Jesus. Why are we given the armor of God if we refuse to go to battle, if we refuse to engage the enemy?

There is a single woman, "Ruth," who, some years ago, was in Uganda as a missionary. She went as a secret agent woman (if you will). She worked at a mission school on an island called Lingira. (It is one of the fifty-two Buvuma islands in Lake Victoria.) The school came under demonic attack, and some of the girls became suicidal. Others were manifesting in strange ways.

Our secret agent was raised in a small country church that didn't teach about spiritual realms, let alone prepare the congregation for facing the evil realm head-on. When things got serious, Ruth retreated to her room for refuge. She was afraid to engage and felt unequipped to do so. Besides, she reasoned, *the local pastors are rallying around the school. They can deal with all this.*

All was safe and snug in that small room (with the door shut) until she heard the voice of God in her spirit: "Ruth, if you do not engage in the battle, you shall not share in the victory!" That personal revelation became her rally cry. She grew a spiritual backbone and (as the boy David did with Goliath) ran into the fray. She personally knew these girls and took them under her wings to pray through their deliverance.

What followed was a great victory. Many of the girls had been delivered, saved, and baptized! Now Ruth has a testimony, and she experienced becoming an overcomer. Takeaway: secret agents do not cower before the enemy. They courageously take back the ground from the enemy!

I am told that a new Northrop Grumman B-2 Stealth bomber costs the US government over a billion dollars! I suppose that you could get in one and, by taxiing, get from one end of the air base to the other, (like a shuttle service) but that is not what it is designed for. A used, one-thousand-dollar golf cart can get you from one end to another. It would be a deplorable use of a billion-dollar aircraft, *right?*

If you are a believer in Jesus, His life, His resurrection, His love, His forgiveness, His power, and His compassion, *you* are *His* B-2 bomber. He is in the control tower (of Heaven) telling us we are clear for take-off. So . . . take off! Once you are in the air, you are not alone. Since you have received the Holy Spirit, He is the Pilot, the Captain. God is not your co-pilot; you, at best, are His!

We are the bomber that the Captain is directing to various targets. That could include sharing the secret of God at a store that is, literally, called Target! Maybe it is Kroger, maybe a Buc-ee's gas station, maybe the library, or at work, or via the internet. The targets are all around us.

The air base is your church. It is there to protect you from the enemy and resupply you before you go on your next mission. You're on the ground for a time, but you're built for the sky! Don't be afraid to fly. You were always meant to fly and engage targets. The sky is the world around you. *Remember Isaiah?* "Those who hope in the Lord . . . will soar on wings like eagles." **(Isaiah 40)**

We know it is not safe. We know that enemy aircraft and Satan's surface-to-air missiles want to take us out. But we know the Captain will safely get us to our target, and we look ahead to where He's pointed us. We don't keep looking behind for the bogeys that are out there.

The Captain's radar is much more sophisticated than ours. He's tracking them. He's sending out His angel flares to conquer the heat-seeking fiery darts of the enemy. We just need to be willing to leave the ground, leave the security of the four walls of the churches we attend, our temporary hangars.

Every day brings us one day closer to Armageddon. (It may be in our lifetime, it may not. Only God knows). We can fly only so many missions before the Day of the Lord or our death (whichever comes first). There will be massive casualties on that Day such as the world has never seen. The only ones spared are the ones we engaged to know Christ, to be known of Him, and to make Him known to others.

I DARE YOU to be an agent of God's secret—to share that secret with everyone you're supposed to share it with. We are the only secret society (on planet Earth) I know of whose task is to share the secret with as many as will listen to us.

> "The new birth is a secret none can know except those who have it. . . . It is a secret that is revealed by the Holy Ghost in the heart. The . . . world would like to know this secret—it would like to know how to get rid of sin."
> **– William Fitch**

> *His body, which is the church, of which I became a minister according to the stewardship from God which was given to me for you, to fulfill the word of God,*

*the mystery which has been hidden from
ages and from generations, but now
has been revealed to His saints. To them
God willed to make known what are the
riches of the glory of this mystery among
the Gentiles: which is Christ in you, the
hope of glory. Him we preach, warning
every man and teaching every man in all
wisdom, that we may present every man
perfect in Christ Jesus.*
– **Colossians 1:25-29** (NKJV)

May you, with the Captain's direction, be the best secret-sharer you can be, whether you whisper it in a hospital, speak it in an elevator, or shout it from a street corner. **May you** hit every target by the trajectory of the Holy Spirit.

REMINDER: We are not victims of our circumstances; children are. We, as adults, are victims of our choices. *Choose wisely. Choose Holy Spirit.*

9

ONCE SAVED, MAYBE SAVED

I CAN'T BELIEVE we're looking at a subject that has been debated for centuries, yet here we are! You and I won't get any clarity until we answer the question: *Is God God, or am I god?* If we answer: "God is God . . . alone," then we have to act as though that's 100 percent true. The minute we try to shoehorn our judgments about people (that God has made in His image) is the moment we fail to live up to "God is God alone." We will have jumped ship and acted like that person's judge, jury, and executioner. The fact is people who come to Christ can make mistakes afterwards.

But, Mike, I know people that used to love God and faithfully attend church or even be in ministry, but they are now both-feet-in to the world, the flesh, and the devil. Therefore, they can't be saved, Mike. **Hebrews 6** *says they have* "fallen away" *and* "it is impossible for those . . . to be brought back to repentance." *That means they are lost forever, Mike. There's no way to sugarcoat that.*

Wow. Is that your final answer? Then why did Jesus tell the parable of the lost sheep? **Hebrews 6** uses the term *fallen away*, but isn't that the same as *run away*? And isn't that what lost sheep do? They run away. In **Matthew 18**, Jesus says there are a hundred sheep in the pasture and one gets lost. It wanders off . . . strays . . . gets out of Dodge.

Now, there are ninety-nine faithful, contented sheep left in the "green pastures" and "beside quiet waters" we read about in **Psalm 23**. *What does the shepherd do?* He doesn't write off the sheep that went astray. Rather, the Good Shepherd goes off into the hills looking for it! When he finds the sheep, "he is happier about that one sheep than about the ninety-nine that did not wander off."

So what's the *why behind the what?* In this case, Jesus is that Good Shepherd, and His *why* is explained in **Luke 19**: "For the Son of Man came to seek and to save the lost." That's God's *why*. You see, the hundred sheep do not represent all of mankind. That's the unscriptural doctrine of *universalism*.

No, that pasture was full of (saved) sheep, not sheep and a few (unsaved) goats. But one sheep must have thought life would (somehow) be better alone, like a goat . . . doing her own thing. In **Hebrews 6**, Jesus (as the Word of God) is telling us this: *He has to be the One* *to bring the sheep back.* Not us. That is not our lane. We can pray for that lost son, daughter, parent, friend, neighbor, or whomever, but that is where our lane ends. **Hebrews 6** is right; it is impossible (for us) to bring that person to repentance again. *Not happening.* But as we read **Hebrews 6** through the lens of **Luke 18**, we clearly see that "what is impossible with man is possible with God." So we commend that lost sheep to God and leave the results to Him. Period.

Years ago, an Oregon believer by the name of Forrest Teal explained the wayward nature of sheep. In view of the fact that sheep live in herds, it boggles the mind as to why one would venture off alone, but they do, as seen in **Isaiah 53**. "All of us," Mr. Teal said, "like sheep, have strayed away. We have left God's paths to follow our own." Mr. Teal drew two circles to make his point.

The following graphics show how our human nature is like that of sheep.

Most sheep stand at the fence line, thinking the grass is greener on the other side, even when it is not. They are not looking to the shepherd (in the center).

But the sheep of His pasture direct their attention to the Shepherd as their all in all. They aren't prone to wander anymore because it can't get any better than being with Jesus. If they do wander, Jesus is their Advocate before the Father (**1 John 2**) and will go looking for them. We can be sure that, whatever Jesus goes looking for, He will find. *Amen?*

Once you're sealed by the Spirit (**Ephesians 1**), you're sealed. *End of story.* Another backup for that is **1 Corinthians 6** where those who are united with the Lord are one spirit with Him. If you're one spirit with God, how (in the world) do you separate that? *He's God.* We put WAY too much power on our ability to think we know what the hell we're doing (at any level).

Mike, if you're really a believer, you wouldn't be doing . . .

Oh, so now it's back to behavior? Back to the Law? Now it's not a gift anymore (as we're told in **Romans 6**)? Well, Jesus said you'll know them by their fruits. That's back to *behavior.* Besides, who's the "them" Jesus is talking about? *You? Me?* No, He's talking about false prophets and exhorting His followers to discern a true prophet from a false one by seeing what these prophets are stirring up in people. He was not deputizing His disciples to start fruit inspecting everyone they meet. *That is not our lane.*

That only leads to pride, legalism, and division. Charles Spurgeon once said: "He who grows in grace remembers that he is but dust, and he therefore does not expect his fellow Christians to be anything more; he overlooks ten thousand of their faults, because he knows his God overlooks twenty thousand in his own case. He does not expect perfection in the creature, and, therefore, he is not disappointed when he does not find it."

That's another way of putting what Jesus preached during the Sermon on the Mount. "Do not judge others, and you will not be judged. You will be treated as you treat others. The standard you use in judging is the standard by which you will be judged. And why worry about a speck in your friend's eye when you have a log in your own? How can you think of saying to your friend, "Let me help you get rid of that speck in your eye," when you can't see past the log in your own eye? Hypocrite! First get rid of the log in your own eye; then you will see well enough to deal with the speck in your friend's eye."

Let's say you grew up in a house with your dad. It's Friday, a school day, and you get your grades today. At noon, your dad texts you: *"How does your report card look?"* You emphasize the good parts, but (at the end of your text) you let him know you got a D in math. *No response.* When you get home later, you go to the door and find it is locked. (That's never happened before.)

You find a note on the door and it's in your dad's handwriting. It says: *"Son, you cannot live here until you get at least a B in math."* Did that ever happen to you? *No.* Why? Because your ability to live with your father wasn't conditioned on you being perfect and getting all A's on each and every report card.

The standard to be achieved (for living with your dad) is *his* love, not *your* behavior. If it were up to your behavior, then you (and not the father) would be determining who stays and goes.

God, our heavenly Father, determines who abides with Him, He doesn't cede that right to us by letting our behavior call all the shots. He is so far beyond that, it isn't funny. Yet we act like we can work around what He already decreed.

From being a high priest to being homeless, you do not have that right or ability. If you did, then God is not God; then He is always on the defensive—looking to see when you have done enough bad things to be *voted off the island.*

The fact is that vote has already been tabulated and it's 3-0 in favor of all saints spending *eternity with the Trinity* in Heaven. We are both powerless to try to affect an outcome God has ordained and stupid to think we could ever get away with it. When we cheapen sovereign, righteous judgment, we cheapen God, and I ain't going there!

Guys, there are a lot of verses that speak to eternal security of the believer and a passel of verses that can be taken the other way. Is Mike a theologian? No. *Thank God.* It's the theologians that argue over these things. No, I am like you: I seek the truth and want to live my life by the truth, not by error or misinterpretation of the truth.

The Word of God is true, and it is our final authority in ALL that pertains to life and godliness. *Amen?* There are multiple times more verses that have just the one condition of salvation: faith/belief, versus what we read in places like **Hebrews 6**.

I DARE YOU to let Jesus be Jesus alone, just as we said God is God alone at the beginning of this chapter. Jesus is our only Judge. We stand only before Him. If you see someone in Heaven that you think shouldn't be there, you can rest assured that some others are thinking the same about you and about me. We praise God that they were not the arbiters of our eternity because they would have given us a one-way ticket to Hell.

"Judging others makes us blind, whereas love is illuminating. By judging others, we blind ourselves to our own evil and to the grace which others are just as entitled to as we are."
- Dietrich Bonhoeffer

Why, then, do you judge your brother or sister? Or why do you treat them with contempt? For we will all stand before God's judgement seat.
- Romans 14:10

May you have confidence, as a believer, that nothing can separate you from the love of God. Because, when you mess up and walk back towards God (with your tail between your legs), He is running towards you to kiss and hug you like the father of the prodigal. We are like books, and Jesus judges us by our cover (which is His cross and empty tomb). He does not judge us by any (or all) bad chapters within. Because all He sees is His righteousness, He judges us accordingly.

REMINDER: We are not victims of our circumstances; children are. We, as adults, are victims of our choices. *Choose wisely. Choose Holy Spirit.*

10

MY NEW BRONOUNS

BEFORE I SHARE the details about this (actual) word, we need some simple English terms defined.

A noun is a person, place, or thing. The sentence *Mr. Smith goes to Washington in a bus*, has all three—a person, *Mr. Smith*; a place, *Washington*; and a thing, *a bus*. A pronoun is a term that describes a person, place, or thing without using the name. If we were to add to the italicized sentence above, we could say: *He wants to get there by noon*. Obviously, "he" refers to Mr. Smith. That pronoun lets us know that Mr. Smith is a guy, because *he* refers to males, just as *she* refers to gals.

Without getting too deep into sociology, I want to make a point that it is important for us to identify one thing from another, be it words, sounds, or things we observe. For the latter, take clothing, for instance. By observing people's clothing, we can identify whether they are a nurse, firefighter, cook, construction worker, ballerina. softball player, and so on. Clothing helps us make accurate judgments about whom we see and how we are to react to them.

If you get pulled over by a police car and a cheerleader (with pompoms) skips up to your car and asks you for your license, you can be pretty sure you're not dealing with a real cop.

God's Word makes the same point with clothes *and* sounds. King Solomon describes an encounter between a young man (in the street) and a loose woman in **Proverbs 7**. He describes her in **verse 10**: "Then out came a woman to meet him, dressed like a prostitute." All the way, back beyond 931 BC, everybody could tell a hooker by what she wore. It was easy-peasy. Not so easy today, as we see how some females dress at the malls.

In **1 Corinthians 14**, the apostle Paul makes another key point by asking two questions: "Even in the case of lifeless things that make sounds, such as the pipe or harp, how will anyone know what tune is being played unless there is a distinction in the notes? Again, if the trumpet does not sound a clear call, who will get ready for battle?"

In other words, if a bugler plays taps (during the day) instead of a call to arms, the soldiers will be solemn, thinking a comrade is being laid to rest. They won't be swiftly getting their gear ready for battle. Shame on the bugler that plays the wrong tune at the wrong time. It could have devastating consequences.

Paul was pointing out that we can't make good decisions or judgments without making accurate *distinctions*. People's clothes help us make reliable distinctions as to their occupations and/or their gender. How people wear their hair has, for centuries, been a symbol of masculinity or femininity. Since time began, facial hair has been the clincher between the two sexes.

Words help us with distinctions too. Specifically, gender pronouns: **he, him, his, himself and she, her, hers, herself**. This reliable vocabulary of gender distinction faces *extinction* with the advent of the dangerous practice of allowing humans to self-identify as their non-biological gender. That's where a biological Sally decides *she* wants to be called Steve from now on, perhaps until "Steve" gets a draft notice from the army or *his* auto insurance goes way up because of the existential gender bias in that industry.

As if that isn't silly enough, the new civil rights push (for our day) isn't equality for minorities but is to ensure that people get to choose what pronouns *they* want to be addressed by. Going beyond a passing fad, this practice has wormed its way into corporate America—going from optional to near mandatory!

Maybe you're like me and wonder why God's Word refers to the Holy Spirit as *He*. Clearly, the most feminine characteristics of the Godhead are evidenced by the Holy Spirit—the Comforter, the One who nurtures us and leads us.

Holy Spirit does not have the Father role or the Son role, so I wonder if we call Him "He," how does that fit? It goes back to the Godhead being a "They," right? They . . . are One. As we say in the Shema (**Deuteronomy 6**): "Hear, O Israel: The LORD our God is one LORD." (KJV)

Recently, I saw a doctor about my neck. When I checked into the hospital out-patient area, they gave me a form to fill out. The form asks, "What gender were you born?" I wrote "Male." Next, it asks, "How do you want to be referred?" (I can't believe I'm reading this), and I wrote "They." So I take the filled-out form to the receptionist, and a woman (she, her) goes through the form to make sure everything is filled out. The intake person says, "You would like to be referred to as *they and them*?" I said, "Yes, I would, ma'am. I want you to call me *they*." *She* replies, "OK." I said, "Stop a minute. *Are you kidding me?* Are you actually having this conversation with me?"

The woman was all business and replied, "*Sir*, I'm just following protocol and rules . . . " I said, "Stop. Ask me why I want to be referred to as they." *She* said, "*Sir*, that's none of my business." My reply? "I'm asking you to make it your business." *She* goes along with that: "OK, why would you like to be referred to as *they*? I said, "Because the Father, the Son, and the Holy Spirit live inside me, so they're three and me—that's four. We're *They*, so that's why I want you to refer to me as *they*." *She* looked at me and says, "Oh my goodness, I follow Jesus as well. That is the most amazing response I've ever heard in my life!"

I'm a *They and a Them*! Those are my *bronouns*. You want to talk pronouns? Call me *They*. "I have been crucified with Christ, and I no longer live, but Christ lives in me. The life I now live in the body, I live by faith in the Son of God, who loved me and gave himself for me." (**Galatians 2**) The Triune God is one God, but with me, we're *They*.

So am I a they and a them now, according to the narrative that's pushed on American society? If that's the case, I guess I'm a they, but I'm really a *he* because that's the way God made me at birth and HE determined my gender all along the way. Period. *End of chapter.*

I DARE YOU to embrace your new bronouns, *they* and *them*, and use them to minister life to others.

> "You can't change the hand that you were
> dealt. The fact is, there's only one deck
> and only one dealer, and you are neither."
> **– Craig D. Lounsbrough**

There is neither Jew nor Gentile, neither slave mor free, nor is there male and female, for you are all one in Christ Jesus.
– Galatians 3:28

May you be wise to never engender gender politics, yet have compassion on those who do.

REMINDER: We are not victims of our circumstances; children are. We, as adults, are victims of our choices. *Choose wisely. Choose Holy Spirit.*

11

IT'S ALL ABOUT ME

WHEN WE SAY, "It's all about me," we're being prideful, and when God says, "It's all about Me," it's being humble and loving. Believe me, it was not all about Jesus as He hung on that tree. It was all about you and me, *not Him*. That's a big bite for us to swallow, but imagine what it was like for the chosen disciples of Jesus.

I was thinking about how the apostles (two thousand years ago) were fishing, doing their jobs, and trying to play their role in each of their families. Every week they (religiously) went to their "Sunday school," or synagogue, and learned about the Messiah, that the Messiah is going to come back some day *(obviously, not in their lifetime)*.

All of a sudden, they meet this unique man and He declares: "I'm Him." Think about this: they're living their life, going about their day-to-day, expecting the Messiah's coming is in the distant future. Then one day, they realize *He's here. It's us! What? No, it can't be us. That's sometime in the future. No, it's now. It's us.* What a shocker.

Talk about a shift! Talk about a revelation and break-through! Did they have any idea how their lives would never be the same again? What were they saying about Jesus around the dinner table? How were they able to wrap their mind around the Messiah calling them by name to follow Him?

Scripture reveals other people that faced incredible shifts in their lives and their concept of God. We'll look at a Jewish girl, a shepherd boy, and a multitude of Hebrew slaves to see what God was doing and the things they went through.

Hadassah was the name given by her parents, but we know her as Esther (in the book of **Esther**). She was a nobody, a young, orphaned woman in a foreign land called Shushan. About this time, the pagan king was looking for a replacement for his outgoing queen, so a beauty contest was held. Mordecai, Esther's older cousin (and father figure), entered her in the royal beauty contest. God's favor was all over her, and Esther ended up winning! However, she had no idea she would stand in the gap to save her nation. She had no clue. That was not what she signed up for, but that's why God made her queen "for such a time as this."

After Esther was coronated, her king was tricked into issuing a decree to make any Jew in his kingdom a target for extermination. Mordecai was a Jew. Esther was a Jew. (You do the math).

In the end, Esther risked everything by going to the king (uninvited). We read that and go: *Big deal. She went up to her husband on his throne.* Everybody, it WAS a big deal. Nobody just walks up to this particular king uninvited. But as we said, Hadassah was a nobody, right? She wisely took her time to make her confession (I'm a Jew) and request (please don't let us be killed).

The genocide kingpin was a right-hand man to the king named Haman, who had a forty-foot gallows made just for Mordecai! (We won't go into the *why*, but just know that it was personal with Haman).

In the next two days, the king not only put a stop to the genocide but also turned the tables. In doing so, Haman was executed, the Jews were saved, and Mordecai went *from gallows to governor.*

Prior to Esther's time, **Genesis 37** introduces us to a middle-schooler boy named Joseph. He had ten older half-brothers. (That, alone, is hard to wrap our minds around, right?) Those guys were on a cattle drive (of sorts) with Dad's flocks of sheep while Joseph (the "baby") stayed home with Mommy and Daddy. One day, his dad sends him on an errand to take some provisions to his half-brothers. BTW, those guys hated Joseph's guts.

Not only was he getting the youngest-child treatment, but also Joseph was the obvious favorite of their dad. He was a burr in their saddle (as we say in Texas), so when he shows up out of nowhere and in the middle of nowhere, the older sibs tie him up and sell him to traveling merchants as a slave! The merchants were heading to Egypt, where Joseph, the fresh, young slave, fetched a good price.

Later, he was falsely imprisoned (for nearly half of his life.). By God's grace, he ended up being #2 man in Egypt, like, the vice-regent of Pharaoh. It was God's plan from the get-go. Had that not happened, a famine (that affected Egypt and all the Middle East people groups) would have caused Joseph's whole family (of future patriarchs) to starve to death in the desert.

Joseph didn't know that. He didn't sign up for that. But it was God. God, God, God, God, God. It was God behind it. God owns it, God controls it, God is sovereign, and Joseph went *from prisoner to prince.*

Friends, the God I'm talking about saw His Son bleed and die on the tree so we could have eternal life. God, Himself, sends His Holy Spirit to us. So whenever we're worrying, "Man, we're in tough times," *guess what?* Tough times yield tough people.

That's why all the Hebrews were strong when they walked out of Egypt. Pharaoh's taskmasters ended up being God's CrossFit trainers, so everyone was physically ready for the journey. They thought their *suffering* was the context. No, their *exodus* was the context; their suffering was *a means to an end*, their ticket to a journey of freedom.

We get so anxious about life when we live it in the absence of understanding God's context.

That was Esther as queen!

That was Mordecai as elder!

That was Joseph as slave!

That was the indentured Hebrews!

That was me at the airport!

Remember, in chapter 3, "Bagless in Monterey," my Pebble Beach experience? If I only knew (when I got off the plane) that my luggage was still at DFW, sitting next to a carousel in a cabinet . . . and that it was safe and I'd get it back . . . if I knew I'd get off the (return) plane, meet an angry woman, then end up in the right terminal, and my bag would be there . . . if I knew God's assignment was this: *Give this airline woman some money and bless her . . .*

Oh, yeah, no problem (I got this, Lord), but I didn't know any of that! All I knew is: *OMG, my luggage is gone! What's going to happen? What am I going to wear all week?* But if I knew upfront, I would have been at peace throughout the week in California and looked forward to the moment of handing the baggage claim gal one hundred dollars.

Everybody, God's declaring: *I'm your luggage. I'm your confidence. It's Me! You don't need to know where your luggage is. All you need to do is know where I am and walk by the Spirit. I will take you step by step. Mike, you ended up getting the bag, and you didn't need to know that upfront. You need to know Me upfront, Mike. You need to know I'm Good. You need to know I wouldn't let you down.*

You need to know there's nothing I would do to harm you. That's all you need to know. Why did you need to know anything else? Mike, all you need to know is I am your God, I am Good, I am your confidence. I am for you—not against you—and I got all the bases covered. Just live your life . . . trusting Me.

Here's what that should have looked like in Pebble Beach: "Oh, hey Mike, where's your luggage?" *I don't know. God knows. He'll work it out.* That's what abiding faith looks like. That's what trust sounds like. That's what a "peace within" feels like. That's a burden-free kind of life, and that's the life I want every day. That doesn't mean I don't crosscheck and verify what I can, it simply means I don't worry.

Esther got that.

Mordecai got that.

Joseph got that.

The Hebrew slaves got that.

A life of faith is agreeing with God in His ways before we experience it physically. It's the Spirit calling the shots for our spirit, soul, and body by overriding our personal will. Even the military teaches us this lesson.

Throughout various wars, you'll find many posthumous Medal of Honor recipients who saved their buddies (in, say, a foxhole) by jumping atop a live grenade while telling everyone else to clear out. *Why did they do such a thing?* How come their will for self-preservation didn't cause them to want to get out of Dodge? *Because their spirit overrode their mind* and a (very natural) fear of death. Their spirit acted far above the fear, not within it! This gave them the opportunity to show "no greater love" for their fellow man by laying their life down for others. It is pure heroism on an earthly scale.

In nanoseconds, those soldiers went from *It's all about me staying alive* to *It's all about me being here, for such a time as this, to save my fellow warriors.* We're not talking army chaplains—who should know they're going to Heaven. We're talking regular men, doing a common thing (being a soldier) in an uncommon way (paying the ultimate sacrifice).

I don't know about you, but that inspires me to a new level. I want a spirit like that, but even better—one led by the Spirit of God because it's all about Him, all about Jesus, all about the Holy Spirit.

I DARE YOU to reorient your thinking from *It's all about me* to *It's all about Him* to see your spirit overtake your mind and body to do His will in His timing.

> "At the beginning of each day, I pray:
> "Lord, today help me find the right
> person at the right time, and say or do the
> right things, for the right result."
> **– Dr. Paul Hatch**

> *May God himself, the God peace,*
> *sanctify you through and through. May*
> *your whole spirit, soul and body be kept*
> *blameless at the coming of our Lord*
> *Jesus Christ.*
> **– 1 Thessalonians 5:23**

May you live your life agreeing with God in the light of God's context and not be chained by the context that our mind tends to go to . . . and be free to walk in the peace that surpasses understanding.

REMINDER: We are not victims of our circumstances; children are. We, as adults, are victims of our choices. *Choose wisely. Choose Holy Spirit.*

12

THE RELUCTANT VISITOR

IN THE BOOK OF **2 SAMUEL**, a man named Mephibosheth ("Sheth") met the mercy of God in a distinct way when he was brought before King David. Sheth met somebody he thought was going to kill him. *Why would David kill Sheth?* Because he was the grandson of the disgraced, and now dead, King Saul, who had preceded David to the throne. In that culture, it was a given that when the new sheriff came into power (as it were), all the relatives of the old sheriff were done away with so they would not have future claim to be in charge (wear the badge).

Sheth was born into nobility. Therefore, he was assigned a nanny. Sheth was a young child when his dad and grandfather (Jonathan and Saul, respectively) were killed in battle as they fought the enemy. When the nanny heard that David had taken the throne, she believed the only thing that was going to happen to this little boy was he'd be murdered. So she picked him up and, in her haste, dropped him, and both of his feet were broken. There was no Mayo Clinic in town, so he became lame for the rest of his life. Since that fateful day, he'd been growing up for seven years (in seclusion).

For seven years, Sheth is thinking, *David is a murderous bastard and no one can let him know I'm alive.* How did he survive this long? Did he change his name? Wouldn't word get around? I can just see a do-gooder approaching the king and saying, *Hey, David, I want to do you a favor. By the way, Saul's grandson is living, and I can show you where he is.*

Eventually, when the king inquires, the king gets answers. The king finally inquired seven years later. He finds out Saul's heir is in hiding in a town called Lodebar. David's men went to Mephibosheth and said, *The king summons you.* What happened next? Did Sheth cry? Did he get sick to his stomach? Was he tempted to flee? Did the people that were taking care of him say, "I love you, master Mephibosheth. I'm sorry about what's going to happen. We'll see you on the other side"? (Because they all know he's going to die.) What other questions could he have asked himself, knowing he's facing the end of his life?

The biggest fear (in Sheth's life) was David finding out about him. Now, his worst nightmare had come to pass, and he's thinking, *I'm going to die. King David is angry with me, the king doesn't love me, the king wants me dead. The king knows I'm an heir to the throne, and his only recourse is to get rid of me.*

Let's pause for a minute. Sheth's belief system led him to judge David's motives (without ever meeting him). In the same way, how many of us believe that our Father in Heaven is stalking us because He wants to punish us for something we did wrong?

You may be thinking: *He wants to get back at us. Our life isn't going the way we thought. God found us out, and He's mean; He's an angry God—and that's why our lives aren't going the way we thought they would. That's why we're not making the money we thought we would make. That's why my marriage is falling apart. That's why my kids are messed up.* Those kinds of thoughts explain how we view God. They will, over time, harden our hearts towards Him.

Let's take it back to the book of **Samuel**. We see Sheth is finally ushered in front of King David, and he bows down (hoping that he can gain mercy by his physical posture). Then, as King David looks at the fugitive, Sheth hears David say the unimaginable: *I made a covenant with your father, and because I made a covenant with Jonathan, I am going to let you live. In addition, you will eat at my table (as though you were one of my sons) all the days of your life.* Suddenly, Sheth was face to face with the total opposite of what his brain had thought about for as long as he could remember.

Friends, *what if we have a similar encounter when we meet the real God in Heaven?* He's the merciful, compassionate, amazing God that punished His Son for you and me. If you connect the dots in this story, Jonathan was Jesus, David was the Father, and Mephibosheth is us.

What did Sheth have to do to save his life? Did he make a covenant with David? *No.* He got to enter into the covenant between Jonathan and David. Our takeaway is that *the covenant* was the difference between life and death for Mephibosheth. Out of that covenant came David's mercy and grace.

It's just as true to say the pre-Creation covenant (**Titus 1** and **2 Timothy 1**) of God's grace and mercy is the difference between life and death for us. *Did we make a covenant with God?* No. *Did we earn our way to Heaven?* No. We enter into a covenant that's already there. Let that sink in and change our life.

A covenant is a solemn agreement between two parties. It is usually meant to be permanent (till death do we part). In **Genesis 15**, we see that the seriousness of a covenant resulted in the sacrifice of an animal or bird. The carcass was evenly split in half and placed on the ground.

The two covenanting parties then had to walk between the two sections of the carcass. The symbolism of severity was unmistakable as each walked between the lifeless creature of God's Creation. The implication is *May God so do to me if I do not keep this oath or covenant.*

The covenant David made with his (kindred spirit) friend Jonathan is referred to in **1 Samuel 18**. Those guys had an "unto death" covenant. It was tested when Mephibosheth was delivered to King David after Jonathan's death. The facts that David was now a king and that his friend had died did not void his oath to Jonathan.

With a covenant, there're no do-overs. It is what it is. Whether you're single or married, young or old, rich or poor, sick or healthy, smart or not so, willing or unwilling, it doesn't change the covenant. We can take comfort in that because God's covenant doesn't change.

We don't go from being saved (like Sheth) by the covenant *today* and have something come up *tomorrow* that makes us unsaved. Yes, we screw up and disappoint God—even to the point of anger, perhaps. Yet **Psalm 30** says: "For His anger lasts only a moment, but His favor lasts a lifetime."

I DARE YOU to live life knowing that God is full of mercy towards you (and NOT wanting to punish you at every turn).

"God loves each of us as if there were only one of us."
– Augustine

But when the kindness and love of God our Savior appeared, he saved us, not because of righteous things we had done, but because of his mercy. He saved us through the washing of rebirth and renewal by the Holy Spirit, whom he poured out on us generously through Jesus Christ our Savior.
– Titus 3:4-6

May you always remember there is a covenant in place for you and live in the light of that.

REMINDER: We are not victims of our circumstances; children are. We, as adults, are victims of our choices. *Choose wisely. Choose Holy Spirit.*

13

FROM RAMSES TO SUCCOTH

GOD IS THE HOLY SPIRIT, but His Word reveals there are other spirits in play. In **Exodus 12**, we see the first Passover in Egypt. The spirit of death (sometimes called the Death Angel) comes one night, and all the firstborn in Egypt not protected by lamb's blood on their doorpost (including Pharaoh's son) die that night.

The plague of death was the final straw for Pharaoh to agree to let Moses take the Hebrews out of Egypt to honor God. That journey of six hundred thousand men (not including spouses and children) led them from the city of Ramses (bondage) to Succoth (freedom), from Egyptian rule to being ruled by the Almighty. It was a permanent Exodus.

To make this truth practical, I need to tell you an accurate account of a man named Scott. One day, he went to his workplace in Oregon, and while he was there, he suffered a severe brain aneurism. That day, Scott went to work in his car, but he left work in an ambulance. At the

ER, they concluded what his condition was. His aneurism left him in a coma.

Here's the backstory. When Scott was about ten, his dad had a condition that led to him being in a coma and remained in that state for years. That took a toll on Scott and his family. It was a strained relationship (visiting his dad), who was kept alive by life support, so the "lights were on," but nobody was home. Scott would talk to his dad, but was he hearing anything? Nothing indicated he was.

Eventually, the dad died, and Scott was left with a firm conviction to never ever have this scenario repeated whenever he had a wife and kids. Therefore, as an adult, Scott had a medical directive drawn up and notarized, stating that if he was ever in a coma and couldn't do this, this, and this, then he must be removed from life support.

Now, Scott's in an ICU bed in a coma, just as his dad was. His family kept a constant vigil in the hospital. Because they believed in Jesus, they prayed. Plus, they put the word out to houses of worship they had attended (over the years), so they could pray too.

There is another dynamic that affects this picture. It has to do with Scott's teenage son. You see, Tyler's last words with his dad were not so nice. He was devastated by the tragedy of what just happened to his dad so soon after their argument. Have you ever experienced something like that? Tyler begged God, "Lord, please just give me five (coherent) minutes with my dad!" He was under heavy conviction to make things right, to say he was sorry, and to ask his dad's forgiveness. *If only . . .*

All too soon, the head doctor approached Scott's wife one afternoon with one of those stainless-steel clipboards in hand. On it was the notarized medical directive. He took Mrs. B. aside, showed her the document, and said, "Here are the benchmarks your husband imposed in this directive. Ma'am, we're not even close. I'm sorry, but we'll have to pull the plug tomorrow or be in legal violation of his wishes. Get your family together today to say their goodbyes." With a heavy heart, Mrs. B. did just that.

Now, I wasn't there, but I can imagine the anguish and sorrow that must have filled that room. The spirit of death seemed to be ever-present, waiting for Scott's body and brain to finally succumb. For the first time, all of the family went home to their own beds.

I don't know many of the details, but the gist of it all is that the next morning Scott woke up! Nobody saw that coming, but God did. The Death Angel got a pink slip and had to leave. If ever the second half of **Psalm 30:5** applied, it applied here: "weeping may stay for the night, but rejoicing comes in the morning." Mrs. B. went from widow to wife, and her kids went from fatherless to fatherful (if there's such a word).

A ton of prayers were answered that day, and the family moved as quickly as they could to get Scott released. He was functional but groggy from the coma experience. Of course, the reconciliation of father and son occurred. The teenager wasted no time, since he now saw a few private moments with his dad as a precious gift.

So what are our takeaways? Probably more than I can list. For starters, we see the truth of God's Word. **Proverbs 18** teaches us that "The tongue has the power of death and life, and those who love it will eat its fruit." The doctor spoke death over Scott to his wife that day. Meanwhile, for days, dozens of saints were speaking life over him to the Lord. Is it any wonder that the fruit of speaking death to people can lead to their death or hasten it?

As humans, from a fallen race, we gravitate to the dark side, the death side. That is why we need the Spirit of God to reorient our thinking to speak life into others. All my books share from the Word and offer teaching on subjects, but beneath all that is my desire to speak life into you and all who read my books and get on my Instagram page (**@mikemoore320**).

I believe that, by doing so, others will want to speak life to their sphere of influence: kids, siblings, friends, co-workers. It takes living under the influence of the Holy Spirit to honor and promote life in what we say and do.

Another Scripture takeaway is that Scott applied past effort (the medical directive) to control a future situation (even though he had no guarantee he would ever face that situation). Turns out he did. **Proverbs 16** (NKJV) declares: "A man's heart plans his ways, but the Lord directs his steps." Scott had a blueprint to have his life terminated, but God established and expanded his longevity (his steps).

And then, Scott got out of the hospital where everything was so controlled. That reminds us of **2 Corinthians 3**: "Now the Lord is the Spirit, and where the Spirit of the Lord is, there is freedom." Scott regained his liberty. He got to leave and get his freedom back. This was a big deal because I left out a *huge* part of what happened when Scott woke up (with zero medical provocation).

Because the physicians couldn't believe what had happened and his mind was a bit disoriented, the hospital was determined to commit Scott to the state mental hospital! Incredible, but true. What's worse is that it didn't seem that Scott, or his family, had any say in the matter.

Somehow, their rights were relinquished and the disaffected medical people were hell-bent to rain on this miraculous parade. Like *God can bring a person back, but not whole.* Thus, the new prayer request (among the saints) was that God would keep Scott out of the insane asylum.

Are you ready for miracle #2? When it came time to transfer Scott to the Oregon State Hospital, the skeptics lost the paperwork! The transfer couldn't legally happen without it, and the family seized that moment of confusion and got their loved one out of there in a New York minute! *Praise the Lord,* right?

My point is this: if we don't live life under the influence of the Holy Spirit, we are so much more powerless. It's like salvation is a cell phone. We always have it with us, but without the Holy Spirit's influence in our thoughts, words, and actions, we're like a phone low on battery, and we're trying to continue using it in the power-save mode.

The screen is harder to see, and some apps (like the camera) will not function. But, in our case, we're in power-lost mode without the Spirit. The power is there, but we're just not plugged into it. Sadly, going to religious churches makes it worse!

Here's the problem with religion. It hands you the flat end of the power cord and says to you: "Plug in to us!" So you do and expect to benefit from the power of the Holy Spirit in your life, but in reality, the *religion* power supply is not plugged into the wall (the true source of power) we call the Trinity. In fact, those religious environments can drain us of what little power we have.

Have you ever plugged your phone in at night (not seeing the whole setup) and had no idea your "5 percent remaining" cell was not getting charged because the cord from the box to the wall got unplugged somehow? The next morning, your cell clock alarm doesn't go off because it lost all power during the night. You skip your breakfast, you're late for work, and your day is a mess because you didn't have the power you were relying on.

People may spend all their life plugged in to religion. Then, when they really need the power of God (in a crisis or at the end of their life), it isn't there. It never was. That's why you are reading this book and why I wrote this book.

I DARE YOU to get out of Ramses and run to Succoth, to the place where God is your all in all, and to speak life to those around you (and to yourself).

> "In whatsoever manner it be, let me turn
> to God and be fruitful in good works.
> Nothing higher exists than to approach
> God more than other people and,
> from that, to extend His glory among
> humanity."
> **– Ludwig van Beethoven**

Finally, be strong in the Lord and his mighty power.
– Ephesians 6:10

May you get, or stay, plugged in to the Holy Spirit. You need that power to thrive.

REMINDER: We are not victims of our circumstances; children are. We, as adults, are victims of our choices. *Choose wisely. Choose Holy Spirit.*

Part III

ROLL YOUR OWN

14

MERCY BEGINS WITH "ME"

THIS TITLE HAS TWO DIMENSIONS. First, it is the vertical mercy we receive from God. It is the mercy He is giving to me. We are mindful of **Lamentations 3** (NKJV): "Through the LORD's mercies we are not consumed, because His compassions fail not. They are new every morning; great is Your faithfulness."

How are God's mercies and compassion new each day? Because this morning's mercies are not yesterday's mercies. As the day ended, those mercies became water under the bridge. Today is a new bridge, a new day for God's compassion and mercy to meet us at our point of need. As the song goes: *The God of the mountains is the God of the valleys.*

If you are in a valley, the Spirit of God stands ready to pour out the love, mercy, and compassion (those three aptly describe the word *grace*). His grace is sufficient for every trial or tragedy you could ever face, even the unthinkable ones, like the death of a son or daughter.

Which brings us to the second dimension of "Mercy Begins with 'Me,'" the horizontal one between humans. In 2006, a twenty-one-year-old woman was killed at an

Oregon apartment complex in a murder-for-hire. Her (real) name was Megan. She struggled with a meth addiction, which put her in the company of questionable examples of humanity. The crime scene was one of a brutal murder.

Megan's father was a presiding judge in Washington County, Oregon. When the three members of the district attorney's office came to his door at 11 p.m. on July 21, he thought they were there to request that he sign a search warrant. Instead, they solemnly let him know that he and his wife would never see Megan alive again. The full account of that personal tragedy is chronicled in a book called *Losing Megan*.

I neglected to mention that Megan's father is a born-again follower of Jesus. His name is Thomas Kohl. That night, the grief train roared into the Kohls' life with a vengeance. It took about eleven grueling months before the police captured the assailant and another two years until the killer (Robert) was found guilty and sentenced to life in prison.

Judge Kohl was at Robert's sentencing as a victim of the crime, not as a judge. At the sentencing, Judge Kohl told Robert, "I forgave you before I even knew who you were." *How could this father say such a thing to this scumbag?* I submit to you that it was because both *Megan* and *Mercy* begin with *Me*. The *Me* in Judge Kohl reminded him of being the unworthy recipient of God's mercy, which allowed him to be both the receiver and the sender of mercy.

That question came up months later when Judge Kohl visited Robert in prison. Shortly after meeting the prisoner, Robert said, "Judge, I am so sorry," as he began to cry. After composing himself a bit, Robert asked, "How can you be so kind to me?" The judge told Robert, "It wasn't me. It was Jesus inside of me being kind," and admitted he could not be this way with him on his own volition. Remember, everybody, Judge Kohl had a choice to make. He chose to forgive in spite of his feelings.

There are some grieving parents so filled with an incessant sense of loss that there is no room for other feelings. That's what Judge Kohl felt. He counts it as a good thing. Why? Because, as he testifies, "I've seen people since then . . . who have ended up being very bitter and angry and resentful. And it just destroys them. It destroys you from the inside out. I was really blessed that I didn't go through that."

Why didn't he go through that? Because *Mercy* begins with *Me*. When he said that Jesus was the One who was being kind to Robert, he was referring to the Spirit of Christ, the Holy Spirit.

In this chapter, we were introduced to an heir of King Saul we nicknamed Sheth. Sheth was allowed to live because of a covenant David had made with Sheth's dad, Jonathan. But there was another relative of Saul named Shimei. The accounts of his interactions with David are in **2 Samuel 16** and **19**.

The backstory is that David's son Absalom had risen up against his dad and was attempting a coup to become the new king. In **2 Samuel 16**, David and his warriors were leaving Jerusalem to go and fight Absalom and his men. On their way out, a man named Shimei ran up to the procession and cursed David, while throwing stones and dust at the king and his cohort. He called David a murderer and that he deserved this uprising of his son . . . and it even got uglier from there.

Abishai, one of David's mightiest men, asked permission to take Shimei's head off. It would have been a very common transaction in those days, but David didn't let his pride go there. Instead, he chose to believe that God had sent Shimei to humble David and that he might be blessed if he accepted the humbling. Therefore, in Mercy, he forbade any of his men from harming Shimei.

Three chapters later, Absalom was killed in battle, David's crown was preserved, and they were returning to Jerusalem, just crossing over the Jordan River.

And who was the first to greet them? You guessed it, Shimei. This time, he was the poster boy of contrition as he pleaded, "May my lord not hold me guilty. Do not remember how your servant did wrong on the day my lord, the king, left Jerusalem. . . . For I, your servant, know that I have sinned." Again, Abishai sought to put Shimei to death. In Mercy 2.0, David forbade him and told Shimei, "You shall not die."

But our friend Mephibosheth was there to greet David too. Though he was treated as a son of David, he did not go out with David to face Absalom. David asked him, "Why didn't you go with me Mephibosheth?" Sheth was in an awkward position and said he had saddled his donkey to go, but his servant betrayed him. He went on to say, "All my grandfather's descendants deserved nothing but death from my lord the king, but you gave your servant a place among those who eat at your table. So what right do I have to make any more appeals to the king?" Yet king David had mercy again. Remember, *Mephibosheth* and *Mercy* begin with *Me*.

Don't you love this? We, like Sheth, deserve nothing but death, yet our King, in His Mercy, not only spares our lives but even invites us to His table—as Jesus invited His disciples on the shore of a lake to "come and have breakfast." (**John 21**) Also, in **Revelation 19**, "Blessed are those invited to the wedding supper of the Lamb."

Was David always so Merciful? Well, prior to **2 Samuel** is **1 Samuel**. In **chapter 25** of that book, we find an idiot that spurned David in a different way. His name was Nabal, and it means *fool*. When David was on the run from King Saul (who sought to kill him), David's men were holed out in a wilderness where Nabal and his wife, Abigail, lived. Nabal was a wealthy, successful guy. He had fields; he had flocks and herds. For all we know, he was the Warren Buffett of that land.

For weeks, David's men (just by being there) deterred marauders from attacking Nabal's flocks. One day, David's food supply was getting low, so he sent some of his men to request sufficient food from Nabal to hold them over. Nabal's reaction was to insult David (though not to his face) and to send the men away empty-handed.

When they told David what Nabal said and did, David flew into a rage! By an oath, he swore to kill Nabal and every male that belonged to Nabal by the day's end. *Folks, this was serious.* David took four hundred men with him to ensure the annihilation he desired for Nabal.

Somehow, a servant of Nabal's got wind of the coming destruction and ran to tell Abigail, his master's wife. She was the level-headed one. She immediately saw the gravity of the situation and had the servants pack two hundred loaves of bread, two skins of wine, lots of grain, five butchered sheep, one hundred cakes of raisins, and two hundred cakes of dried figs. All this she sent ahead of her coming out to meet David.

She got herself ready and proceeded to a ravine on her donkey. David and his men were just entering it when she got off and bowed down to David. Next, she fell at his feet and said, "Pardon your servant, my lord. . . . Please pay no attention to that wicked man Nabal. . . . As for me, your servant, I did not see the men my lord sent. . . . let this gift . . . be given to the men who follow you. Please forgive your servant's presumption." Then she went on to praise David, speak life and blessings to him and death to his enemies.

After she was done, David said: "Praise be to the Lord, the God of Israel, who has sent you today to meet me." David did call off the death and plundering of Nabal.

Days later, Nabal died anyway, and David praised God again: "He has kept his servant from doing wrong and brought Nabal's wrongdoing on his own head." So we see that if Abigail had not intervened (and David had acted on his anger), David would have been doing wrong, or evil. *The opposite of Mercy is doing wrong.* David always had the opportunity to fail, but God sent Abigail to give him an opportunity to show Mercy and succeed in God's eyes.

[Side note: Nothing in Scripture describes Abigail as a beauty to behold. If you continue reading **1 Samuel 25**, you'll find that David married Abigail after she was widowed (a pattern that would follow him later).]

You may be a single woman reading this book. Perhaps you are despairing that you aren't a looker as some count attractiveness. Just know that it wasn't Abigail's looks that attracted the king to her. It was her character and humble heart. She generously gave food to David's men. Not just fifty cakes of figs, but two hundred! Good character and uncompromising integrity are guy-magnets for many men.

But, Mike, wasn't Abigail saving her own posterity by saving her husband?

Of course, she had skin in the game. One cannot lose a husband (especially in that culture) and not feel the effects. Her lane was to save her husband's life. She succeeded. Nabal died of his own evil. David may have pitied her, but he first was blessed and impressed by her actions and words. In short, her character and spirit.

Back to mercy. Actually, we never left mercy because Abigail had mercy on her husband. Perhaps you are married and your spouse is a jerk or a fool or a fraud of some sort. You may have your own Nabal to deal with each day, cleaning up their messes and the fallout from their outbursts of anger, their addiction(s), whatever. That's a tough life, and I'm sorry if that's the lane you are in (like Abigail). Just know that *Mercy* begins with *Me*.

I DARE YOU to acknowledge the past mercies God has shown you and your family and to look for future mercies—as they are new every morning.

"When it comes to humans, mercy is hard to come by. Not so with God. His mercy is like a huge bucket of water filled to the rim so that if you bumped into it, it would spill all over you. His mercy is so great the he doesn't just forgive us when we fail, but he erases any record of our failure. He doesn't just reduce our sentence— eternal punishment—he eliminates it and sets us free."
– Craig Groeschel

Blessed are the merciful, for they shall be shown mercy.
– Matthew 5:7

   May you live in appreciation of vertical and horizontal mercy. In other words, be a good receiver and a good giver of God's Mercy. Mercy begins with you. Mercy begins with Me.

REMINDER: We are not victims of our circumstances; children are. We, as adults, are victims of our choices. *Choose wisely. Choose Holy Spirit.*

15

NO DROUGHT ABOUT IT

THIS CHAPTER IS ABOUT WATER, not the kind of water you drink from a bottle or a brook. It's water as a symbol of something greater. Jesus speaks of this water to a Samaritan woman He met at the well of Jacob.

She came to draw, and He said to her: "Everyone who drinks this water will be thirsty again, but whoever drinks the water I give them will never thirst. Indeed, the water I give them will become in them a spring of water welling up to eternal life." (**John 4**)

You may know that, prior to what He said, He had asked the woman to give Him a drink. That's when the cultural bias kicked in. Her response went beyond a simple yes or no. Instead, she said, "You are a Jew and I am a Samaritan woman. How can you ask me for a drink?" Jesus did not get into that Jew/Samaritan thing with her (and that serves as a lesson for us). He would play neither good cop nor bad cop. Instead, He spoke to her on a spiritual level: "If you knew the gift of God and who it is that asks you for a drink, you would have asked him and he would have given you living water." (**John 4**)

Her ultimate plea to Jesus is: "Sir, give me this water so that I won't get thirsty and have to keep coming here to draw water." (**Verse 15**) At the time, she was probably pulling her container up from the well by a rope. Thus, the activity of her hands affected her head—so that she asked Jesus for the ability to never thirst.

He wasn't going there. He was deep into spiritual truth, dealing with the eternal, when she kept gliding on the surface, dealing with the temporal. Basically, she was distracted by the cares of this world.

Jesus was inviting her to another world, His world, His kingdom, where the Holy Spirit empowers believers to keep His commandments, not to earn His love but *in response* to His love. Do you see the difference?

Jesus is the Living Water. In a sense, He is saying to the woman: *Take Me into you and you will never thirst for:*

love,

compassion,

hope,

security,

faith, and much more.

My water, My Spirit, will flow out from you, and you will drink freely. That is consistent with **Matthew 10**: "Heal the sick, raise the dead, cleanse those who have leprosy, drive out demons. *Freely you have received; freely give.*" [Emphasis added.]

As this woman wondered, how can we drink of this Spirit? We are told, in **John 7**: "Whoever believes in me, as Scripture has said, rivers of living water will flow [out] from within them."

This is why we experience dry times in our walk with the Lord. We stop sensing His presence. He doesn't seem to respond to our prayers. The Scriptures seem abnormally lifeless, and we feel we're stuck in a desert of estrangement from God and not lying in His green pastures and by His still waters.

So we pray for more of Him, more of His presence in our thoughts and lives, more of sensing the warmth of His love. We pray for a deeper indwelling *of* the Spirit or sensitivity *to* the Spirit. We pray for a breakthrough, but God does not answer that prayer. Why? *Because He already has!* If you love Jesus, then rivers are to be flowing out of you. You are experiencing (or have experienced) what could be described as a *reverse mirage*. It's not that you see water that isn't there, it's that you aren't seeing water that is there!

We don't see and experience that living water because we are used to drinking water as it flows IN (like drinking from a hose or water fountain). But your new fountain isn't plumbed that way. You need to drink as it is flowing OUT. *Can you see the difference?* We're called to be rivers, not reservoirs, of the Holy Spirit! Being a reservoir causes us to thirst because we're not flowing to others. It is a one-way ticket to leanness in our soul.

The solution? Open the spillway of God's Spirit in you, and let it flow to others. Then your thirst will be satisfied because you will be satisfying the Lord, who sees your water flowing and blessing others. It has always been God's way. You need prayer? *Pray for others.* You need resources? *Give of your resources.* You need to hear cheerful, energy-giving words? *Speak to someone else that way* and see the Lord provide for you.

What did Jesus say? *Rivers of water will flow out from within My believers.* This is not a rule to get into Heaven. This is God's way to quench your thirst on Earth. He knows you have needs here. He wants to be in constant fellowship and communion with you, but we get off track and look for a spring when *we are the spring,* or river of life—as evidenced by the Holy Spirit bearing fruit in our lives.

Jesus did not shame the woman. He told her the truth about Him and offered Himself to her. She was so overwhelmed by Jesus that she ran back to town to encourage everyone who would listen to her to come see the Messiah. That's how I want to roll, by being so overwhelmed by Jesus every day that I just want to bring other (thirsty) people to Him.

I DARE YOU to be that overflowing fountain Jesus made you to be. Are we to be ministers of reconciliation, according to **2 Corinthians 5**? *Absolutely!* But that ministry is designed to float on the living water flowing out from within, His Spirit coming from within you and out of you.

> "If a spring has not been opened in a
> soul, a spring of living water from God's
> own Son, no waters can flow and there is
> no life in you."
> **– G. V. Wigram**

> *Give, and it will be given to you. A good*
> *measure, pressed down, shaken together*
> *and running over, will be poured into*
> *your lap. For with the measure you use,*
> *it will be measured to you.*
> **– Luke 6:38**

May your harvest of God's goodness and power flourish as you water the fields of others, that they may reap a harvest too.

REMINDER: We are not victims of our circumstances; children are. We, as adults, are victims of our choices. *Choose wisely. Choose Holy Spirit.*

16

THE PRODIGAL AND THE PRODIGY

THERE'S A PARABLE Jesus tells in **Luke 15** about a man and his two grown sons. Parables were like reality TV in Jesus's day, only not so lame. In parables we hear of people going through *real life* situations. That's why people listen and relate to the characters and the trials they face in the parables.

Jesus doesn't tell this story to point out a dysfunctional family. This account is a means to demonstrate the unconditional love of God. *Why would Jesus tell such a story?* Because His audience didn't know the love of God, and neither do we. We don't know the love of God. We just don't know the fullness of it! It surpasses our length, height, and breadth, and it's like He loves us *that* much.

In this story of the prodigal son, the father looked for the prodigal. He didn't go to the far country. He waited for him to come back, looking in the direction his son would take to come home.

What did the father say when the prodigal came back—*Son, you spent all my money . . . ?* No, he said to his helpers: *Put the robe on him and put a ring on him. He was lost and now he's found.* That's it. The broken man had it rehearsed: *Father, your servants eat better than I. I'll just be another servant . . .*

You're my son; you're back home, was his dad's reply. He never brought up what the son did. Maybe that came later, like: *Hey, what did you do when you were out there?*

Dad you're not going believe what I did.

The father didn't have to go after him about that. The son, based on the immense amount of love heaped on him, may have said: *Dad, can I share with you what I did? I was eating the best food. I had women, wine, I had everything. Then I had no more money, and I had no more friends.*

Then, the older brother says to the father: *What are you doing? Why are you being nice to him? I've been in this home this whole time. You never prepared a special meal for me . . .* The dad says: *Son, it's been here all along for you. But you are so angry. Why are you so angry?*

One man's behavior could not be condemned in a court of law. The older brother did everything right. (That's religious people today, but their hearts are far from God.) The prosecutors have nothing to go on because they can't see inside the man, but God can. For instance . . .

I can walk up with a gun and put it to a man's head, and the police would be around me saying: "Sir, drop the weapon. Sir, drop the weapon." As long as I don't pull the trigger, I don't go to jail for murder. But God says: *You already murdered him in your heart.* That's the difference. That's the older brother. He did everything right but had murdered his brother in his heart.

Our Father God deals with both sides. He loves the religious and He loves the rebellious. He loves the prodigal and He loves the prodigy. There's no difference.

What about the young son? Doubtless, there were witnesses that could say: *We saw him in the brothel. We saw him looking at pornography. We saw him getting drunk. We saw him lying, cheating, stealing, gambling, and buying prostitutes. We should stone him.*

Friends, I'm telling you the truth: I'd rather be him than the older brother. *Why?* Because the older brother has to get like his kid brother before he can see the truth and begin to know the depth of God's love.

The older son always had his father's love, but he took it for granted or didn't grasp how to walk in that and love others. For both the prodigal and the prodigy, it was all about them. That was one thing they had in common.

If I asked you where the love chapter is in the New Testament, you would be quick to say **1 Corinthians 13**, right? "Love is patient, love is kind. . . . It always protects, always trusts, always hopes, always perseveres. Love never fails." That chapter excellently explains what love is.

The **Luke 15** account is a love-explained-by-actions chapter. It shows us what "bearing all things, believing all things, hoping all things" (quoted above) looks like in a challenging situation. The older son didn't push the envelope of his dad's love as the younger one did.

Had he done so, we could expect a similar, loving response from the father. Which brings me to the conclusion that we don't have to push God to discover that He loves us. But when we hang around God, at whatever distance we care to, the amazing love of God can seem routine to us.

The problem with a free gift (salvation) is that we tend to disregard those things that are free—as opposed to when it costs us something . . . maybe a lot. The prodigy took his dad for granted, and the prodigal took him to the cleaners (so to speak).

Both sons needed to trust in their dad's love more. They just came to it at different angles. I can't think of a wrong way to get to God's love. The only thing we can do wrong is not receive it when it's offered, and it's offered now.

I DARE YOU to go from the shallow end of man's love pool to the deep end of God's love. That's where He'll be.

> "One who has been touched by grace will no longer look on those who stray as 'those evil people' or 'those poor people who need our help.' Nor must we search for signs of 'loveworthiness.' Grace teaches us that God loves because of who God is, not because of who we are."
> **– Phillip Brooks**

> *The LORD your God is with you, the Mighty Warrior who saves. He will take great delight in you; in his love he will no longer rebuke you, but will rejoice over you with singing.*
> **– Zephaniah 3:17**

May you catch the vision of being God's delight and one that He rejoices over because He loves you so much.

REMINDER: We are not victims of our circumstances; children are. We, as adults, are victims of our choices. *Choose wisely. Choose Holy Spirit.*

17

TEMPLE-DRIVEN LIFE

OK, MIKE, WHAT'S A TEMPLE-DRIVEN LIFE?

Well, for clarification we look at **1 Corinthians 3**: "Do you not know that you are the temple of God and that the Spirit of God dwells in you?" (NKJV) That's how Jesus understood it. In **John 2**, the Lord is speaking with His detractors in the (physical) temple of Solomon: "Jesus answered them, 'Destroy this temple, and I will raise it again in three days.' They replied, 'It has taken forty-six years to build this temple, and you are going to raise it in three days?' But the temple he had spoken of was his body."

If we understood we are a temple of God, how would that affect us? How would that alter the way we make decisions? How would that change our life? It's cool enough to be a temple, but we don't merely exist as an empty temple because the Spirit of God dwells within us. Think about it. We're not just a temple of beauty (external) but also a temple of substance (internal), the best of both worlds! A temple with the Holy Spirit residing can totally affect your decisions because you have a purpose and a Person guiding you.

Have you ever visited a temple? Millions of people visit temples each year. Some make pilgrimages and suffer through long lines and torrid temperatures to visit temples in Mexico, temples in India, temples in Japan, all sorts of temples. The Jerusalem Wailing Wall is the remnant of the last Hebrew temple of God. *What do you think draws people to temples?*

The majesty?

The history?

The peace or serenity?

A sense of being or purpose?

The desire to feel God's presence in a special way (like a connection)?

You expect temples to be filled with shrines, statues, candles, incense, and music. There's an awe folks experience at temples because they're different. They point people to a simple, peaceful life. They allow visitors to imagine a different life, a spiritual one!

We, as temples, are called to have the same effect (as physical temples) on those we come in contact with (our visitors). They are not expecting to visit a temple, but according to **1 Corinthians**, that's exactly where they landed . . . at a temple . . . at YOU!

So, as good temples, we don't point them to God through architecture and shrines (exterior things); we point them to God by reflecting His Spirit and loving personality within us (interior things). The foundation of our temple is Jesus, and Jesus is love!

That is why the apostle Paul wrote in **1 Corinthians 13**: "If I speak in the tongues of men or of angels, but do not have love, I am only a resounding gong or a clanging cymbal." OK, I get it. Lots of temples do have resounding gongs, but maybe that's to remind us that traditions and rituals have replaced love in those places. A loveless temple shouldn't expect any return visitors, and that may be a lesson for our temples.

We don't *have to* work at being a temple of God; *we are* a temple of God—and that realization will motivate us to fill it with the best things. What's at the top of the *best things*? That's to be filled with love. A love that is shared. Love that is kept is a love of self. It bears no fruit. It doesn't give or show others how to give.

As you get more practice at remembering you're the temple of God, already filled with His Spirit, emanating the love of God, emanating the peace of God, emanating the mercy of God, and blessing those around you, you'll find that people will go out of their way to visit your temple again and again because their first visit was so pleasing.

Guess what? Though some people will be attracted to the exterior of your temple (with their eyes), it's the interior of your temple that will speak volumes (to their heart). They will see that you are in "others" mode.

Conversely, when we are in "self" mode, we automatically suppress the Spirit. That causes us to do and say things that can put off those around us. But when we purpose to yield to the Spirit, *we change*—and that change is obvious to those around us. They want to visit our temple of God because it's safe, it's respectful, it's comforting and even fun!

Remember, we're talking about us being a temple of God, based on **1 Corinthians 3**—how that equips us to a temple-driven life—and that life is freely given to us!

Hear what the apostle Paul says in **1 Corinthians 2**: "What we have received is not the spirit of the world, but the Spirit who is from God, so that we may understand what God has freely given us." *What's "freely given to us by God," everybody?* It's the fruit of the Spirit (**Galatians 5**) and the gifts of the Spirit (**1 Corinthians 12**).

Let's talk about the fruit of the Spirit. Like me, have you ever said: *I need more patience, I need more joy, I need more love?* Really? You were given all the fruit of the Spirit when you accepted Jesus as your Lord and Savior. That fruit was deposited in you. All you have to do is uncover what's already there—not ask for something from the outside (when you already have it on the inside).

How about the gifts of the Spirit? Words of wisdom, words of knowledge, faith, healing, miracle acts, speaking in tongues, interpreting tongues. They're just that—gifts. We have things freely given to us by God: fruit and gifts.

Now, **1 Corinthians 3** makes more sense. To paraphrase: *Everyone, don't you remember? Don't you know that you're a temple of God? And that **all** of the Spirit dwells in you; the One who gave you all those gifts, the One who gave you all that fruit? He gave those to you. Don't you know that? Never forget.* Let's focus on the fruit of the Spirit and the gifts of the Spirit.

Imagine going to a wedding reception. As you enter the hall, you're handed a food plate. You're excited and anticipating really nice food. Walking past an overflowing gift table, you approach a long, cloth-covered table, but instead of food there, you see just a bunch of cardboard boxes on top!

Now, you kind of wish you weren't holding the plate. *What's the point?* Your confusion leads to frustration, and just as you're about to ditch the plate somewhere, the host scrambles to the table and lifts each box to reveal the most delicious fruit trays underneath!

You didn't know it, but there was one box for each guest. Your name was on the back of your box. All you had to do was lift it up to receive the fruit that was prepared for you.

And that massive, overflowing gift table? There were gifts with your name on them as well—free for the taking, but you didn't know that. You assumed they were for someone else! Friends, this chapter was written so you could discover your fruit and gifts by living a temple-driven life under the influence of the Holy Spirit.

Remember, all the fruit was already deposited inside your spirit, and the gifts were already given to you. Jesus has prepared a table (of fruit and gifts) for you on Earth, as well as the Marriage Supper of the Lamb table in Heaven. (That's why we celebrate the Lord's Supper on planet Earth). Receive with joy what is yours for your blessing!

I DARE YOU to not just harbor head knowledge (that you are a temple of God) but to also live that out with the Holy Spirit as your resident. Part of living that out is to believe the fruit of the Spirit and gifts are for you . . . not for someone else you think deserves them.

> "God is in the midst of fashioning
> His temple out of His most precious . . .
> people. You are part of that temple, being
> built into a structure that exactly adheres
> to God's specifications."
> **– Derek Prince**

*What agreement is there between the
temple of God and idols? For we are
the temple of the living God. As God
has said: "I will live with them and walk
among them, and I will be their God and
they will be my people."*
– 2 Corinthians 6:16

May your temple radiate the goodness of God to the point that a visit to your temple is a visit with the Holy Spirit.

REMINDER: We are not victims of our circumstances; children are. We, as adults, are victims of our choices. *Choose wisely. Choose Holy Spirit.*

18

SINNING IN THE SPIRIT

IT SOUNDS LIKE A CONTRADICTION in terms because it is. In the book of **2 Samuel** is the account of King David and Bathsheba. If you've read **chapters 11 and 12**, you know that David had sex with another man's wife and later had that man killed (in battle).

Here is my list of the wrong things David did: First, as a king, he should have been leading his army in battle. He wasn't. Instead, he sent his commander Joab to fight his battles. Remember chapter 6, "We Are All Trans"? Because David didn't do what he was supposed to do (as a king), he transgressed. He was trans.

Second, while he was in the wrong place at the wrong time, he observed a voluptuous woman bathing from his palace penthouse. It wasn't a mere glance. I believe he *stared* at her. We have a word for that. It's called *voyeurism*!

Third, after feasting on her with his eyes, he had a very selfish thought: *I must have her!* So he inquired of his staff about who she was and sent for her to be brought to him. We have *two* words for that: *human trafficking!*

Fourth, she (a married woman) was brought to the palace, and King David had sex with her. That (of course) is textbook adultery! She conceived a child as a result of this one-night stand—as her husband was one of many fighting David's battles for him. She got word to David that she was preggers (as the English say). He started to panic but devised a plot (or workaround).

This is where things get even darker! He ordered General Joab to send Uriah (the husband) home from battle. Certainly, David assumed that Uriah, being a man and married to one of the hottest babes in town, would have sex with his wife ASAP. But David didn't know the character of his soldier, the depths of Uriah's integrity.

Uriah didn't have relations with Bathsheba. He complied with the orders to come back, but in deference to his comrades-in-arms, he refused to set foot in his house and sleep in his own bed—and everybody knew it because he slept in the quarters for David's servants. The next night, David got Uriah drunk, supposing he would forget his conviction, but Uriah still did not go home.

When David realized his scheme had failed, he remembered that in the Mosaic Law (referenced in **Romans 7**) a wife is bound to her husband so long as he is alive. But if he dies before her, she is no longer bound to him. A spirit of death (evidently) came over David, and in that spirit, he wrote a letter to Joab and sealed it.

We call such a letter a *hit job* because in it, David commands Joab to ensure that Uriah is killed in battle— that he dies by the enemy's hands. And who did David choose to deliver this letter to the commander? Uriah! He was told to do it, and as a good soldier, he did what he was told.

[Side note: Sometimes we recruit others to enable us to engage in our sin. First, David used his servants to bring Bathsheba to him, then there's Bathsheba herself, then he co-opted Uriah into coming home, and then he sent Uriah back to the battlefield with his own death warrant, which brings us to Joab, who carried out the plot to kill one of his key warriors.]

Sure enough, the deed was done, and word came back to David: *mission accomplished*. Bathsheba was notified. She grieved but then soon took up residence in the palace as David's new wife. At last, David's initial selfish desire was satisfied. The woman he *had to have* became his wife, and he could have her anytime he wanted.

Everything was rosy until the prophet Nathan paid David a visit. He told the king a parable about a rich man who had his servants slaughter and dress a poor neighbor's only lamb because company was coming. That story enraged David: "As surely as the Lord lives, the man who did this must die! He must pay for the lamb four times over, because he did such a thing and had no pity." **(2 Samuel 12)**

After the king's pronouncement, Nathan immediately said: "You are the man!" **(Verse 7)** Later, Nathan also said: "Why did you despise the word of the LORD by doing what is evil in His eyes? You struck down Uriah the Hittite with the sword and took his wife to be your own. You killed him with the sword of the Amorites." **(Verse 9)**

This rocked David to the core because now he could look back on all he had done and see it from God's perspective and not David's perspective. He was a broken and contrite man. He was assured by Nathan that he would not die (as David, himself, had pronounced on the man in the story). However, the male child Bathsheba gave birth to *would die.*

In the midst of his brokenness, David wrote **Psalm 51**. Here is a limited, verse-by-verse summary:

v. 1 Have mercy on me, O God.

v. 2 Wash away all my iniquity and cleanse me from my sin.

v. 3 For I know my transgressions. [*See, I told you he was trans.*]

v. 4 I have sinned and done evil in Your sight.

v. 7 Wash me and I will be whiter than snow.

v. 10 Create in me a pure heart, O God, and renew a steadfast spirit within me.

v. 11 Do not cast me from Your presence or take Your Holy Spirit from me.

We'll stop there because I want to point out how important it was to David that the Holy Spirit not be taken from him. Implicitly, he is saying he could not have done all those things (we read earlier) if the Holy Spirit was abiding in him and affecting his thoughts, words, and actions.

Absolutely true . . . in the First Covenant. *But what about now?* You are a professing believer in Jesus and you pull a David (in some measure): a selfish or lustful thought, a sexual fling, bringing others into your mess, whatever. **1 Corinthians 6** says your body is the temple of the Holy Spirit, but your body was involved in what you know was a sin. *How can this be?* Do we await a punishment like King David? Is there the Christian equivalent of *bad karma* coming your way?

I say no. Even, no way! *Why?* Because the blood of Jesus covers you. *Period.* Some people see that as a blank check to sin without consequences. I see it as the Lord's open-door policy without guilt. The penalty for your sin is a check Jesus has already cashed. You can't cash it again! You'll go nuts trying. I know . . . I've been there, done that.

King David had come-and-go Holy Spirit experiences, and he yearned for the Comforter Jesus promised His eleven disciples. (**Acts 1**) That Comforter is ours for the asking and for the believing . . . and even when we fail to believe we are sealed, that doesn't unseal us! To be honest, you don't have that much power—and neither do I. God keeps His promises even when we drop the ball.

Having the Holy Spirit (in residence) does not guarantee you will never screw up, never sin again. We have a High Priest. His name is Jesus. He intercedes (or pleads) for us at the throne of the Father. **Hebrews 4** reveals (speaking of Jesus): "For we do not have a high priest who is unable to empathize with our weaknesses, but we have one who has been tempted in every way, just as we are—yet he did not sin."

I DARE YOU to know (without doubting) that the Holy Spirit doesn't evaporate the minute you mess up. Let those defeats motivate you, as a blood-bought believer, to be reminded the Holy Spirit is in you and loves you.

> "In my experience, take the Holy
> Spirit out of the equation of your life and
> it spells boring. Add it into the equation

of your life and you will never know where you are going to go, what you are going to do, or who you are going to meet."
– Mark Batterson

Who then is the one who condemns? No one. Christ Jesus who died—more than that, who was raised to life—is at the right hand of God and is also interceding for us.
– Romans 8:34

May you rest in the knowledge that the Holy Spirit is not limited by your lack of performance or lack of faith. May your interest in spiritual things grow as you become more aware of that very real realm.

REMINDER: We are not victims of our circumstances; children are. We, as adults, are victims of our choices. *Choose wisely. Choose Holy Spirit.*

19

CONFIDENCE IN CHAOS

RECENTLY, I WAS TALKING with a gentleman from Albania. He's about sixty years in age. His country got free from communist rule in 1991, and he remembers all that. He was talking with me and some dinner guests and sounded really scared. He was almost tearful about this.

With all seriousness, the man said, "Do you realize that America is the last bastion of freedom in the world? When America goes down, the entire world goes down." He continued, "I don't want to go back into Communism like I grew up in. You have no idea what that's like, no idea. Americans can talk about it and say, 'Yeah, socialism! Let's go (rah rah), let's get more government control.' Had you lived it, you'd never say that. You'd never say, 'It's not that bad' if you lived under a communist socialistic regime. You'd say, 'OMG, what just happened to us?' We fear what's going on in America because it's a slippery slope right now."

That really got me thinking, and I realized that our only hope is God. Before we look at the incredible hope we have (or *could* have), let's look at what **Isaiah** said about 2,800 years ago.

In **Isaiah 24**, it says: "See, the LORD is going to lay waste the earth and devastate it; he will ruin its face and scatter its inhabitants—it will be the same for the priest as for people, for the master as for his servant, for the mistress as for her servant, for the seller as for buyer, for borrower as for lender, for debtor as for creditor. The earth [will be] completely laid waste and totally plundered."

It goes on and on and on and on and on: "In that day the LORD will punish the powers in the heavens above and the kings on the earth below." Isaiah's just explaining: we have rejected the God of the universe (who made everything); it's in His hands.

Basically, the rulers of the earth (including the United States today) are looking up and giving God the finger, saying, *We don't need You; we'll do this on our own. We'll get along. We don't need the Creator. We're mankind; we will figure this out.* We see a growing number of rich people with an agenda. I'm talking about billionaires that are using leaders (like puppets) to try to achieve their agenda—which is to get away from God.

God says: *You can't do this. You can't live without Me. Earth will not survive without Me. I'm God; I made* it. I made you. *You're trying to live independently, doing your own thing with your own rules and saying you're god. It won't work. If I take my Spirit off planet Earth, the earth will melt. The earth will be destroyed.* God says: *OK, I'm telling you what's going to happen because it's going to get bad before My Son comes back again.* Listen, everyone. God is doing everything He can to help us course-correct to Him and His love.

And Isaiah continues with hope (it's so good): "You will keep in perfect peace those whose minds are [fixed on You] because they trust in you. Trust in the Lord forever, for the Lord, the Lord himself, is the Rock eternal." **(Isaiah 26**) This squares with **Proverbs 3**: "Have no fear of sudden disaster or the ruin that overtakes the wicked, for the Lord will be at your side [your confidence] and will keep your foot from being snared."

Lately, I've been thinking about everything that's going on. Friends (in America), we're slowly sinking into catastrophe. Is the Lord able to send us a president to bring us back to God? Not someone condoning the evil in America, saying, "Everything is OK." It may be some other catalyst that helps this country (and so many other countries) course-correct to both fearing and loving God (again). Make America God-Fearing Again is the appropriate MAGA slogan.

There are many examples of how we are getting estranged from God. Society has been doing what's right in its own eyes for centuries. Today, that plays out as redefining marriage, redefining parental rights, redefining who's a male and who's a female, saying, *I'm a this, I'm a that.* It all just doesn't work. It can't work and never has worked. Society is either agreeing with God or agreeing with someone else. *Who is that someone else?*

Remember, you are God's creation, even though you feel estranged from Him and won't call God your Father. The enemy knows that if you do, he's lost you. In truth, you can't call God your Father; you can only call Him your Creator if you've not come to Christ to become God's son or daughter.

The enemy knows that. (BTW, he'll always hate you because you were made by God, whether you believe in God or not.) But we don't see that destruction (mentioned in **Isaiah**) coming because we're sitting in our own world saying: *It's all about me. It's all me.* Folks, when I say, *It's all about me,* it's pride (on my part). When God says, *It's all about Me,* it's humility and love (on His part).

To me, it feels like we're in the middle of a pot full of water, and it's getting hotter and hotter. You remember the analogy of putting a frog in a pot of water. If it's hot, the frog will immediately jump out. But if you put the frog in neutral water and turn up the heat gradually, it will not sense the change and will eventually get boiled to death. *Is that happening in our society right now?*

This is what I sense God is telling you and me: *Here's your life, Mike. Go out and do your business with excellence. Don't judge people. Love the person I put in front of you, and walk this out on planet Earth. People will see that; they'll be edified, and I'll be glorified.*

That's the Spirit-filled life. It's: *Lord, I'm here. You're God, I'm not. I'm the lesser, You're the greater. I'm looking at You. I may think I know something, but I don't really know anything, Lord.*

What if we go through this tumultuous time where freedom dies? Suppose freedom in America is gone. *What if?* Maybe it won't be gone. Maybe we'll get a reprieve for another ten years or fifty years. *But what if?* God says: *Mike, rejoice. Be glad I chose you for this time. Enjoy this . . . I'm with you. I'm not making a mistake. I know whom I put on planet Earth and in what generation. I know what I'm doing. Stop worrying!*

The mistake we made is that we (collectively) ate from the tree of the knowledge of good and evil. We gained a conscience, so *we think* we know right from wrong. We don't know anything! God has to tell us. But we won't hear if we neglect to say things like: *Lord, I can't act independent of You.* When a country tries to act independent of God (with its laws and decisions and ways), how can God bless its people? As a notable

Christian youth worker has said..."God judges nations in history and humans in eternity."

But, in His mercy, God is saying: *Everyone, I've given you the freedom to make choices. Choose to depend on Me so I can step in and shower you with My love and mercy because the enemy is trying to prevent that. He's heating up the water. I can control all the outcomes anytime, but I've given you freedom to make choices. Choose the one path that Jesus has cleared for you.*

When we're not led by the Spirit of God, anarchy is the end result, darkness is the end result, hate is the end result, evil is the end result, death is the end result. There is no other result. The key is to not let that impending result define who we are. It defines only the stupid things our society has done. But as long as God is, there's hope.

When God is *our Father*, when God is *our God*, when He is *our confidence*, when we're walking *with Him*, when the Holy Spirit is *moving us to Scripture* and the Scripture so indwells us that we just become walking love machines, then nothing matters because we have the confidence of our Creator in us, Christ in us, the Hope of Glory. (**Colossians 1**)

Part of the chaos we live in today stems from colleges and universities pushing a *one-world* (let's all be family) utopia. It's not going to happen! We're all different. We're sovereign nations. There need to be borders—

to establish jurisdictions, to enforce laws. People don't think there are sovereign nations anymore. There are sovereign nations! It's the Tower of Babel all over again!

America is handing over our keys of liberty and self-government to our enemies. You don't think they know that the world's last hope for freedom (on this globe) is the United States of America? We're the last hope for freedom. When that hope gets destroyed, the entire world goes down. So when is that day? No one knows. But we hear this . . .

Well, yeah, someday in the future . . . What if that future is now? What if we're the ones walking in it, and God chose us for this time? In chapter 24 of my book, *Love God Get Divorced*, I talk about us being the "fourteenth generation." So let's embrace it because He's our confidence. We don't have to worry about anything. *He's our confidence.* He'll get us through; we just need to trust Him and walk with Him.

I DARE YOU to have total confidence in your heavenly Father. Use that confidence to sail through the stormiest of seas and get through the deepest of valleys.

"We have full confidence in Jesus Christ.
In that kingdom of faith, we are dealing
with Him . . . the one who cannot lie. . . .

Our confidence rises as the character of God becomes greater and more trustworthy to our spiritual comprehension. The One with whom we deal is the One who embodies faithfulness and truth."
– **A. W. Tozer**

. . . being confident in this, that he who began a good work in you will carry it on to completion until the day of Christ Jesus.
– **Philippians 1:6**

May you never EVER question what God is doing and always trust that He's got your back.

REMINDER: We are not victims of our circumstances; children are. We, as adults, are victims of our choices. *Choose wisely. Choose Holy Spirit.*

Part IV

INHALING AND EXHALING

20

THE JESUS FACTOR

LET'S SEE WHAT JESUS DID in the New Covenant. He turned water into wine, raised the dead, healed the sick, fed five thousand-plus, calmed the sea, and cast out demons. After all that, His disciple Phillip said, "Show us the Father and that will be enough for us [to believe]." (**John 14**) Jesus says, "Anyone who has seen me has seen the Father." (**Verse 9**)

That's a HUGE statement right there.

Hebrews 1 says, "The Son is the radiance of God's glory and the exact representation of His being." Therefore, we're talking about not *a replica* but, rather, *a clone* of the Father, which makes sense because Jesus Himself said: "I and the Father are one." (**John 10**)

Looking to **John 1**, we read: "In the beginning was the Word, and the Word was with God, and the Word was God." Jesus is the Word, yet Jesus comes out of Mary's womb and goes through natural growth stages.

Next, we see in **Luke 2**: "Jesus grew in wisdom and stature, and in favor with God and man."

Jesus (though the Son of God) was subjected to the growth process that a human being goes through so He can fully represent man. Although not being a man through the agency of man (with male sperm), He was still fully man. He got to experience growing up, crawling, walking, puberty, and teenage years. He did it to be able to represent mankind before God (which is Himself).

God represented Himself to man by becoming a man. Jesus was the Word made flesh. (**John 1**) He was the walking Torah, right? So, if you wanted to see what God was like, you just looked at Jesus. People looking at Jesus saw what God, the Father, is like: His character, His passion, His love and desire to be in relationship with us.

That is our beginning point of reference, our north star, if you will. Now we know what Jesus did among the people. He lived among them, taught with authority, et cetera. And yes, He ate and drank in the presence of a prostitute. Yes, He hung out with some tax collectors.

The religious mindset might argue: *Yeah, but He made them change what they do.* No, He didn't. Absolutely not! They changed their destructive lifestyle because they met the real Word. They met a merciful, loving, forgiving, nonjudgmental Savior. They met Him and must have gone: *Wow, He is not what we thought.*

He is not like the religious leaders. They met somebody who unconditionally loved them.

We approach the holy God with blood, but the blood of bulls and goats couldn't save forever, which Jesus did to the uttermost. (**Hebrews 7**) He was the final Lamb, the last Lamb, even the last Adam. (**1 Corinthians 15**) He was the One with His one-for-all-time sacrifice. He would put *an end to Hebraic blood sacrifice* because His blood was completely enough.

It was not only the purest blood, but it was also the only blood that offered permanence. As He hung on a cross, Jesus said: "Father into Your hands, I commit My spirit." (**Luke 23**) He decided to give up His spirit, and His body died immediately. Then three days and nights later, He went and resurrected that body. It was all God's plan before the Earth was formed. (**1 Peter 1**)

Sadly, the way many Christians present the Good News of Jesus is a turnoff. It's not Jesus that people are turned off to; it's *the presentation of Jesus* that they're turned off to.

Jesus is the Savior of the world. If we could see Him today hanging out with prostitutes and drinking wine in a pub, the religious would say: *You can't be doing that. It's Sunday. What are You doing? Why are You sitting down? You just had Your third glass of wine, Jesus. That's not what we want to see. We want to see You come in and tell people to straighten up their lives.*

True to His nature, the Jesus I know would say: *I come in and love people. I tell them My Father loves them and that the Kingdom is at hand* (see **Matthew 4**). *I love them unconditionally. They're going to understand, when the Law is written on their heart, that's where the Holy Spirit comes in. It's written on the heart. I've taken out your heart of stone and put a heart of flesh in. I've purposely not written it on tablets of stone like the Ten Commandments. (Been there, done that.) Because if I write My law on your heart and it's a heart of stone, you're back to the Ten Commandments.* (**Ezekiel 36**)

You're obligated to obey them without fault, and you can't. When I write it on your heart of flesh and I put it in you, then that's going to become a desire for you to want to do what's pleasing to Me, and the Holy Spirit will lead you into all the things that I told you about.

Is that your experience with Jesus?

Is the Law of His grace written on your heart—as you yield it to Him?

If not, why not?

Why would you wait another day to enter into that kind of heart and that kind of precious life? If you haven't surrendered all to Jesus, what have you got to lose?

There's no one-and-only sinner's prayer. You won't find that in Scripture. What you will find are people who know they are lost and can't live out the Law of Moses.

You find them asking (repeatedly), *What must I do to be saved?*

Acts 16: The Philippian jailer (broken heart of flesh)

Luke 23: The condemned thief on his cross (heart of flesh and desperation)

Luke 18: The rich young ruler (insolent heart of stone)

Acts 22: Saul of Tarsus (heart of flesh)

John 3: Nicodemus the Pharisee (heart of flesh)

Acts 8: The Ethiopian regent of Queen Candace (heart of flesh)

Acts 2: Three thousand men in Jerusalem at Pentecost (hearts of flesh)

The answer to *What must I do to be saved?* starts and ends with two words: DECLARE and BELIEVE. "If you declare with your mouth, 'Jesus is Lord,' and believe in your heart that God raised him from the dead, you will be saved" (**Romans 10**) . . .

"for, 'Everyone who calls on the name of the Lord will be saved.'" (**Verse 13**)

Peter, at Pentecost, didn't use the words *declare* and *believe*. Instead, he instructed the three thousand seekers to "repent and be baptized, every one of you, in the name of Jesus Christ." (**Acts 2**) He promised them that upon their baptism they would "receive the gift of the Holy Spirit." **(Verse 38)**

Friends, I can't wrap my mind around the word *repent*. It's used over one hundred times in the First Testament, and it means to sigh sorrowfully, to lament over who we are or what we've done. But I like the Hebrew term *teshuva*. It is the main focus of Jews between Rosh Hashanah and Yom Kippur. It's translated in English as *repentance*, but it clearly means *return*. It's like we're running away from Jesus; then we stop, turn around, and start returning to Jesus.

A twelfth century Torah scholar named Maimonides lived out teshuva in three steps:

Regret,

Confession, and

Leaving the sin—evidenced by a commitment to not repeat the sin.

All the people I pointed out in Scripture (earlier) had these three elements, except the rich young ruler. He was a possessions guy. Those were both his idols and identity. So his only regret was that Jesus told him to sell all his possessions and give the proceeds to the poor. He wouldn't go there. That was *a bridge too far* for him. It didn't have to be, but he made it out to be such.

Do you have a bridge too far? Do you have things you hold onto so tightly that you won't let even Jesus pry your fingers away?

So we get saved by declaring (out loud if we physically can) that we believe Jesus is Lord and that He was raised from the dead. You can quietly confess any sins or addictions that have plagued you if you want and thank Jesus for forgiving all that. Show Him you are remorseful for offending or ignoring Him in your life. Unlike the young rich guy, offer Jesus your all in full sincerity.

God says (in **James 4**), "Come near to God and he will come near to you. Wash your hands, you sinners, and purify your hearts, you double-minded."

I DARE YOU to truly come to Christ by putting your idols on His altar and go from calling God "Creator" to calling Him "Father."

> "Believers who are living in close fellowship with God are not going to think about how terrible they are. They will have righteousness-based thoughts that come through meditating regularly on who they are 'in Christ.'"
> **– Joyce Meyers**

> *Forgetting what is behind and straining*
> *toward what is ahead* [a new life in Christ].
> **– Philippians 3:13**

May you give your future to God so He can work with you in the present, having forgiven your past.

REMINDER: We are not victims of our circumstances; children are. We, as adults, are victims of our choices. *Choose wisely. Choose Holy Spirit.*

21

WHAT'S IN A WORD?

OFTEN THE BEST WAY to define a term is by example. Our example can be seen in **Matthew 16**. There, Jesus is taking a poll of His disciples by asking them, "Who do people say the Son of Man is?" Scripture records they basically gave Jesus three answers of who people thought He is: John the Baptist, Elijah, and Jeremiah. Then Jesus goes deep with them: "Who do you say I am?"

In that moment, Simon Peter gets *a word* and replies, "You are the Messiah, the Son of the living God." Jesus answers him: "Blessed are you, Simon, son of Jonah, for this was not revealed to you by flesh and blood, but by My Father in Heaven." So we see that *a word* is a God-inspired revelation, or unction. Peter did not come up with that answer based on rabbinical teachings or the instruction of his parents. That would have been "flesh and blood."

No, Peter got (what we also call) *a download*. He was spoon-fed that answer by the Spirit of God. He did not get an A for the truth of the answer, but he got an A (from Jesus) for *speaking the truth*. That's encouraging because we can get an A for speaking the truth too!

We mustn't fail to remember this high calling: the privilege of receiving *a word* is coupled with the duty to *speak the truth* . . . to share that word when the time is right. By the way, God gets to choose that time.

Recently, I was with some friends. I esteem the husband highly for his gift of being able to connect believers and ministries all over the world, yet by his own admission, he had a problem with his dad. Here is a man so used by his Father in Heaven, but things were not right with his earthly father. Worse yet, there were struggles in this couple's marriage.

That night, God gave me *a word* for him. It was not to preach to him or to give him some sort of command. Rather, the Lord had me ask him some questions:

"Do you want to break Satan's back?" *(He did.)*

"God's Word [**Ephesians 6**] says, 'For our struggle is not against flesh and blood, but against . . . spiritual forces of evil in the heavenly realms.' "Do you believe that?" *(He did.)*

"Is your dad flesh and blood?" *(He said that he is.)*

"So your real struggle is not with your dad, is it?" *(He admitted it wasn't.)*

At this point, the questions stopped and the revelation began:

"So stop right there. Brother, God's calling on your life and your wife's is so great. That's why this attack is so heavy. The way to break Satan's back is to get on an airplane and visit your earthly father.

"Remember, your struggle isn't against flesh and blood; it's against the demonic. Friend, that demonic has you tied up (in your feelings) and you don't even see it. If you want to break the demonic stronghold over your marriage, over your children, over your *whatever*, get on a plane to visit your father. When you see him, say, 'Dad, I need you to sit in a chair.' Then, take a bucket of water, take his shoes and socks off, and wash his feet. As you do so, tell him, 'Please don't say anything. Just listen for ten minutes.'

"'Dad, I want you to know that if I disappointed you as a son, I'm sorry. If I've said anything against you or thought (for a second) that you're not perfect for me, I'm sorry. God caused you and my mother to form me, and I am here to thank you for that. Plus, I want to say I'm sorry and that I love you.' You don't have to feel that, brother; *just say it*, and Satan will fall out of the sky."

When we get a word from God's Spirit, it serves a purpose. That is why we need to share it. Guys, not sharing a word from the Lord is like being married and never telling your wife that you love her. You are not treating her right by God's standards. You miss a husbandly purpose by not speaking to her in that loving way. When this couple told me their marriage could be much better, I was (from the outside) able to discern the root cause. The cause was a demonic attack (against them and their ministry). If the enemy can steal, kill, and destroy their marriage, he will gain the bonus of destroying their ministry. *Right?*

That word, or insight, God gave me was that Satan's foothold on their marriage stemmed from the man's lack of appreciation for his dad. Like lava from a volcano, his lack of appreciation for his dad flowed into a lack of appreciation for his wife! That was bringing her down, stealing her joy, and affecting their ministry!

Do you see the difference between me getting *a word* and sharing it with them as opposed to merely telling them, "Well, I'll be praying for you guys"? (That's our Christian-sounding go-to line, isn't it?) That's not what they needed that night at dinner. They needed revelation, a breakthrough, to *shift* his attitude and throw Satan off his axis. God was (and is) ready, willing, and able to supply that revelation—but He often uses people like us to express it!

That's the difference between Mike Moore giving counsel to a friend and God giving counsel. His is always the best counsel, but it won't come across if we are not obedient to share it.

But, Mike, how did you know it was God's word and not your own?

That's easy, as I look back on it. What I said to them and the *way I said it* were completely over my pay grade! My mind doesn't work that way. It can't. So, the word (or thought) comes, and I say it. In my spirit (during or after), I want to know that it lines up with God's Word because it is the final authority.

I know a couple that lived in Arizona. They were foster parents to children. One day, they came under conviction that they were talking the pro-life talk, but what had they really done with that? How could they put feet to their belief? So they agreed to work with a local Christian adoption agency by opening up their home to care for an unwed mother. She had already made the choice to not abort her baby.

Soon, they got a pregnant eighteen-year-old girl from the Midwest. Her name was Kim, and her story was sadly pathetic. Her boyfriend, Todd, had sex with her and she conceived. When she informed him, Todd decided to write her off and move two thousand miles away from her—to Arizona. For some (internal) romantic reason, Kim decided to go to Arizona and attempt the impossible with Todd *if* she could find him. As if just seeing each other would make everything all right.

So she was taken in by this couple, who had a young son of their own. The agency met with all the young women once a week for counseling and such. One day, Kim was despondent. My buddy and his wife were in the living room when he asked Kim what was wrong. She said she didn't look forward to going to these meetings because "they always emphasize adoption" and she wanted to keep her baby.

Out of the blue (so to speak) my buddy got *a word* and he said to her, "Kim, everything's going to be all right. You are going to have this baby, and Todd will be there at the birth." When Kim heard that, she lit up with joy. She hugged him and hugged his wife and "floated" down the hall to her room.

My buddy looked over to his wife. She was staring at him in disbelief. Finally, she said, "How could you say those things to that girl?" His answer was not too satisfying because he didn't know how it all came out the way it did. Even though he was the speaker, he felt like a spectator to the whole exchange. It was kind of surreal.

But, so many times, that's how it works with the Holy Spirit's unction. We get words (of knowledge) to give words (of comfort, instruction, and joy). As Jesus said:

"'Freely you have received; freely give.'" (**Matthew 10**). There is joy in speaking God's truth to those who need to hear it.

By the way, there are two Greek expressions for the term *word*. The one we're most familiar with is *logos*. That refers to the *written* word. The key logos in our life should be the written Word of God.

The other Greek term is *rhema* (RAY-muh). That refers to the *spoken* word. A rhema is an utterance. Let's look to **John 1:1** and insert the appropriate Greek term. Here it goes: "In the beginning was the [*Logos*], and the [*Logos*] was with God, and the [*Logos*] was God." Here, Jesus is referred to as "the Logos."

So He is not only the express image of God (**Hebrews 1**) but also the Word (Logos) that became flesh (**John 1**). Jesus is the walking Torah, but when He spoke to people, He was giving them rhemas as He spoke truth to them.

Looking to **John 15**, Jesus tells His disciples (and us): "If you remain in me and my [*rhemas*] remain in you, ask whatever you wish, and it will be done for you." In **Romans 10** (NKJV), we read: "So then faith comes by hearing, and hearing by the [*rhema*] of God." *Isn't that interesting?*

If you read the Word of God, you are taking in the logos. But if you read it out loud and someone hears you, that person is receiving a rhema, a holy utterance. At times, we *get and share* rhemas. Other times, we *hear and receive* rhemas. Logos and rhema are like sunshine and rain. God uses both to grow us.

Before we go to the Dare, whatever happened to Kim? Did she ever see Todd again? Well, she had a healthy baby girl named Kyrra Desiree. And yes . . . Kyrra's father (Todd) was at the birth! (Hallelujah!) Friends, when God gives us *a word*, it shall come to pass. He makes no mistakes. Whatever He says, we can take it to the bank.

I DARE YOU to be both a receiver and sender of words from the Spirit of God.

> "Having your spiritual radar up in
> constant anticipation of His presence—
> even in the midst of . . . chaos and regular
> rhythms of your everyday living—
> is paramount in hearing God, because
> sometimes the place and manner you
> find Him is the least spectacular you'd
> expect."
> **– Priscilla Shirer**

Jesus answered, "It is written: Man shall not live on bread alone, but on every word [rhema] *that comes from the mouth of God."*
– Matthew 4:4

May you be ready in season and out of season to get a word and use that word to minister to the person God intended it for.

REMINDER: We are not victims of our circumstances; children are. We, as adults, are victims of our choices. *Choose wisely. Choose Holy Spirit.*

22

HOLY SPIRIT AS COMFORTER

PSYCHOLOGISTS STUDIED YOUNG CHILDREN and monitored a portion of their brain called the amygdala. In an adult, the amygdala is about the size of an almond, and it controls our fight-or-flight response to life situations. More accurately, it's fight, flight, or freeze. The amygdala is tiny but so powerful that it can control our whole body!

The psychologists showed kids some scary face images of people that looked angry, mean, or sad. Of course, it was unsettling to the toddlers, and their amygdala monitoring captured that. After taking a break, they sat the kids back down, but this time their mothers were brought in to sit next to them.

The moms weren't allowed to talk to or touch their kid. As a few more scary/dramatic faces were shown, the monitored data confirmed that the youngsters were much more comfortable with their mom alongside. That catalyst for added comfort is called *buffering*. It changes the chemistry of the amygdala, which changes our responses and outcomes.

Next, teenagers were assembled to play a video driving game. They had opportunities to make dangerous driving decisions. Routinely, they took unneeded risks, such as running red lights. Their amygdala activity was duly noted.

After a break, they also sat a parent down next to the teen. Same rules: no talking or touching. *You know what happened?* The teens quit running the red lights! They were not as likely to do the risky and reckless things that would bring certain damage to their car. That, too, was *buffering*. Both experiences in buffering the amygdala had positive results.

What does that have to do with the Holy Spirit? EVERYTHING! Your amygdala is a part of your physical brain. If the Holy Spirit is in you, you now have a working spiritual brain. That spiritual brain comforts, soothes, and buffers our physical brains—just like the moms being a comfort to their kids. The moms were not allowed to control their young, but just being there kept them from slipping out of control, out of sorts, anchorless. The Holy Spirit is the Comforter standing next to the children . . . and we are the children.

184 / Love God Get High

The Holy Spirit buffers our fears, our doubts, and our despairs. In **Isaiah 41**, God says: "'Do not be afraid . . . do not fear, for I myself will help you,' declares the LORD, your Redeemer, the Holy One of Israel."

That's an "I will" promise from God. When we are in a situation where we're about to fight, take flight, or freeze, we don't need to try to fix our amygdala. We just have to soak in the presence of the Lord by His Spirit and let all the holy buffering take place in our spirit, mind, and soul.

Jesus is the one who first described the Holy Spirit as our Comforter in **John 14**. Two chapters later, He said it's needful that He leave the Earth so the Comforter would follow. He wasn't just being humble; He was aware that the Spirit's lane was to evangelize the world. Jesus's lane was to destroy the works of the devil, perform signs and wonders, personally choose/equip key disciples, then suffer, die (for you and me), and rise again to ascend to be with the Father till He returns to rule and reign for one thousand years and win the final battle of Armageddon. **(Revelation 20)**

"He will teach you all things AND remind you of everything I have said to you." (**John 14**, all caps added) This is so important because . . . *when do we need a Comforter?* When everything is calm and under control? *No!* It's when everything seems to be coming apart at the seams and fears come (from within and without) that we need a Comforter.

Take persecution, for example. In **John 15**, Jesus advised his followers that the world would hate them "'because it hated me first.'" Therefore, Jesus prepped His disciples to be captured, imprisoned, and dragged before councils regarding their faith in Him. *Guess what? They were!*

We get to sit in on His teaching by reading **Luke 12**: "'When you are brought before synagogues, rulers and authorities, do not worry about how you will defend yourselves or what you will say, for the Holy Spirit will teach you at that time what you should say.'"

Jesus isn't saying, *Don't worry; be happy.* He's saying not to worry because your best defense will come from the Comforter. There are many things that you *could* say but only one thing that you *should* say. At that point, things may not seem to go our way, but we can be assured they *will* go His way. This assurance spares us from judging ourselves in hindsight: *If only I had said (this or that).*

In **Acts 7** we see this played out with Stephen, the martyr. Jews were in the synagogue disputing with Stephen, and he aced them on each topic. When they saw there was no contending with him, they got some false witnesses to say that Stephen blasphemed both Moses and God.

That caused a *real* insurrection, and Stephen was arrested and brought before the Sanhedrin, where he made his defense before the High Priest and the ruling council (and a mob). By the Spirit, he laid out a terrific account of Hebrew history that included Abraham, Jacob, Joseph, Moses, David, and Solomon.

All hearts (in that place) were in solidarity with every word Stephen spoke about the past. But when he brought it to the present, it got ugly. Here is what he said to all who were listening: "'You stiff-necked people! Your hearts and ears are still uncircumcised. You are just like your ancestors. You always resist the Holy Spirit!'" (**Acts 7**) Then, he got even more direct: "'Was there ever a prophet your ancestors did not persecute? They even killed those who predicted the coming of the Righteous One [Jesus]. And now you have betrayed and murdered him—you who received the law that was given through angels but have not obeyed it.'" (**Verses 52-53**)

The crowd was so cut to the heart that they became maniacal, baring their teeth at him. But Stephen was so full of the Spirit that he looked up to Heaven and saw the glory of God. "'Look,' he said, 'I see heaven open and the Son of Man standing at the right hand of God.'" (**Verse 56**) Everybody, you know that after Jesus ascended into Heaven, He *sat down* at the right-hand of God. (**Luke 22**) But look at what is happening here. Stephen is about to become the first martyr of the body of Christ. He will be killed for his faith. That meant so much to Jesus that He stood up from His throne and let Stephen see the hope of His glory. THAT IS POWERFUL!

Like two-year-olds not wanting to hear a parent's command or instruction, the crowd covered their ears to shut out Stephen's words, then yelled at the top of their lungs, and rushed at him. In a word, *mayhem* or *malevolence*. By force, they dragged him out of the city for one purpose: to stone him to death. Those wearing long sleeves took their garments off and left them with a young man named Saul—who went on to become the apostle Paul (after he got a word from Ananias in Acts 9).

Of all the targets on the backs of the mob and the leaders (dull of hearing, hard of heart, etc.), Stephen went for the biggest target in his remonstrance. Do you remember what it was? "You always resist the Holy Spirit."

Sadly, that observation holds water in most churches today. Folks, if we are not embracing the Holy Spirit, we are *resisting* the Holy Spirit. It's that simple. It's like we're in a glorious ballroom in Heaven. The music is playing, and the Holy Spirit is across the room smiling at you. You've already danced with the Father and the Son but not the Spirit.

There He is, still smiling, still waiting as the music plays, but you haven't budged an inch! He is yours to dance with, but you have to ask Him to dance and then let Him do the leading.

In **Acts 25**, the apostle Paul had made an appeal to go before Caesar, or the Jews would kill him. In **Acts 26**, Paul was preliminarily brought before King Agrippa and Queen Bernice. We can be sure that Paul was in the Spirit as we read his words (uttered that day). Paul proceeded to honor the king, and he shared his testimony of being healed of blindness and getting saved!

The encounter concludes with this exchange between Paul and the king: "'The king is familiar with these things, and I can speak freely to him. [That's liberty, BTW.] I am convinced that none of this has escaped his notice [That's confidence.] because it was not done in a corner. [That's openness.] King Agrippa, do you believe the prophets? [That's a faith challenge.] I know you do.' [That's affirmation.]

"Then Agrippa said to Paul, 'Do you think that in such a short time you can persuade me to be a Christian?' Paul replied, 'Short time or long—I pray to God that not only you but all who are listening to me today may become what I am [a disciple of Christ], except for these chains.'" (**Acts 26**)

Who was in control there? Not the king and queen. Not Festus the governor, not even Paul the prisoner. The

Holy Spirit (as Paul's Comforter and Teacher) was in control of that dialogue. Since the Spirit was in Paul, he was not begging for his life as most prisoners would have done. Instead, he used his limited time to minister and attempt to lead a king to Christ!

As being yielded to the Spirit of God, Paul's mission wasn't to save his life; it was to save the lives of all the others in the room. Paul was speaking truth to disarm the dirty bomb of Satan's deceptions and save everyone around him that he could.

We are God's sheep, Jesus is our Shepherd, and the Holy Spirit is His rod and staff. I get that from **Psalm 23**: "Even though I walk through the darkest valley, I will fear no evil, for you are with me; your rod and your staff, they comfort me." This is a chapter about the Comforter, and this book is about the Comforter, the Holy Spirit.

I DARE YOU to let the Comforter have sway with your thoughts and words, not just when the promise of persecution comes upon you but in regular times as well. Having asked, in faith, He is with us.

> "God has called me and has been my
> pilot. The Holy Spirit has been my comforter,
> my guide, and my power source."
> **– Reinhard Bonnke**

*And I will pray the Father, and He shall
give you another Comforter, that He may
abide with you for ever.*
- John 14:16 (KJV)

May you rest in knowing the Comforter has come to calm the seas of your emotions, the volcanoes of your confusion, and any feelings of exclusion.

REMINDER: We are not victims of our circumstances; children are. We, as adults, are victims of our choices. *Choose wisely. Choose Holy Spirit.*

23

SINNERS IN THE HANDS OF A LOVING GOD

LIFE IS LIKE A ROLLERCOASTER RIDE with God. He's in the front car going, *Woo hoo!* And we're petrified, saying, *Lord, can You slow it down?* He says, *I'm about to speed it up. Hang on!* He's not speeding it up to torture us. He wants us to see how fast we can go when we hang on (with both hands) to Him. We'll never know how far (and how fast) He can take us if we let go.

It's our loss, not His, if we let go . . . don't trust . . . and act on our fears. Sure, God would rather have us not bail, but that doesn't make Him angry.

Seriously, most people think God's angry. One cause may be that famous Jonathan Edwards sermon entitled "Sinners in the Hands of an Angry God." Spoken to his congregation in Massachusetts, this 1741 message was pivotal to ushering in the First Great Awakening in America. But here's the deal: God is happy. He's a happy Creator. He's not pissed off. Since our sins were dealt with at the Cross, it's *His redemption of our sin* that makes Him smile. He's got it all covered. His plan has been that way since the beginning.

Having said that, if we were to ask a group of believers (in a room) to describe the look on God's face as He looks at us, we would be inclined (if we were honest) to describe His face as mildly disappointed. His expression would seem to say: *Mike, you could do a little bit better.* But that concept of God is a lie from the pit of darkness.

If our picture of God looks like that, we are not in tune with the Father's heart and either we never climbed in God's rollercoaster, or we let go at some point. It starts with acknowledging that God exists, but it can't stop there. **Matthew 25** shows a guy who did let go.

In this parable, the master gave each of his three servants different amounts of money. One went out and invested, doubled the money, and gave it all back to his boss. Another one went out and invested, doubled his portion, and also gave it back to the boss.

But when the third one came along, he said, *I knew you were a man who reaps where he doesn't sow. I knew you were like that, so I just buried it, and now I'm giving back to you only what you gave me.* The master said, *You're evil for thinking that way. At the very least, you should have put it in the bank to earn a little interest.*

Why was the last servant called "evil" or "wicked"? Because he projected *his own vile character* onto his master and foolishly accused the master. [Side note: people are doing the very same thing with God today.]

That servant saw his master as *exploiting*, but the other two servants reveal to us that the Master was actually *enabling*. He was setting all three servants up to succeed, giving them the seed money to work with. I look at that as a 0 percent interest business loan—to learn to buy and sell with someone else's money so they might wisely invest their own money someday.

The worthy servants applied their time and talents to the task and made bank. They hung on to their master (like in a rollercoaster ride). The unworthy servant buried his loan proceeds. When he did that, he was letting go of his master. In doing so, he made *nothing* from *something* (that's called destruction), which is the opposite of God—who makes *something* from *nothing* (that's called creation).

Part of hanging on to God (for us) goes beyond allowing God to direct our steps. It has the look and feel of earnestly desiring that God lay out our future in His loving, giving way. But we (stubbornly) want to work for it all. So God says, *You want to work for it, instead of trusting Me? You don't need Me? You want to do it in your own strength, instead of riding on Mine? That's a decision I give you the freedom to make.*

We will always go farther with God, but if we're too stubborn and insist on the *fight-for-every-inch* path, at best we'll do OK in life because there's a natural law of sowing and reaping. Armed with such a (me, myself, and I) worldview, we blindly enter the rat race of working hard (in our own strength) for what God was holding out to us on a silver platter by faith in Him.

God just wants to bless us. He wants us to be His kids. It's like He's saying: *Would you sit still and let Me just shower you with My blessing? Can I do that for you?* But we often block Him: *No, you can't do that; it's not fair!*

Friends, God is not a God of fairness. We don't want God to be *fair* with us. Otherwise, we'd get the punishment we deserve, and grace becomes extinct! No, in wisdom, we seek His grace and His favor.

So, Mike, is this a chapter about a prosperity gospel? Is that the takeaway?

No, it's a chapter on the favor and Fatherhood of the best, loving, compassionate, slow-to-anger God. He wants us to prosper (**3 John 1**), but financial success is a *ripple effect*, not the object that hits the water and starts it all in motion.

Pastor and author Randy Alcorn said: "God prospers me not to raise my standard of living but to raise my standard of giving." God prospers us to be conduits of His love for others. When He stops loving, then we can stop . . . but He'll never stop, so neither should we.

Let me demonstrate God's kind of prosperity with a true story of a married couple in Mexico. Born and raised there, both the husband and wife grew up to become medical doctors. But rather than have lucrative practices in the city, they, as Spirit-led Christians, moved out to a remote village (called San Andres Tlayehualancingo) in the Puebla mountains to serve the small community there. *Cool, huh?*

Full disclosure: I never met this couple. What I am sharing here comes from their son Alejandro. Alex (as he's known in the States) was a ten-year-old boy when this story unfolds.

His mom was in her last trimester of pregnancy in that village when a natural disaster occurred in Mexico. Hurricane Gilbert ravaged the Mexican landscape. Trees were blown down, power was cut off, and rivers flooded their banks. Because of the latter, this mountain village became unreachable. No one could get in and no one could get out!

At that time, Alex's mom experienced late-term complications with her pregnancy. Being a doctor, she knew she needed to get to a hospital for an emergency C-section, but that was impossible. She couldn't even be packed out by mule! The only way out was by helicopter, and the airports throughout Mexico had grounded all flights due to the hurricane they called Gilberto.

At last, the winds had passed, and there was even a ray of spotty sunlight upon the village. But things got progressively worse for the expectant mother, and the village's whole (faith) community got together in a school building to pray for a miracle to save her life and the life of the baby.

As they were praying, they heard a noise (outside) getting louder and louder. It was so unusual that the people stopped praying and flocked outside to see what it could be. To their amazement, a helicopter lowered onto the school basketball court (about the only flat area in that village). In minutes, the pilot and a well-dressed man came out of the helicopter.

The first words out of the pilot's mouth were "¿Donde es ciudad de Zacatlan?" (Where is the city of Zacatlan?) The villagers all pointed southwest. It turns out the man in the suit was the secretary of the Interior in Mexico. He heard about the devastation in Zacatlan and ordered the helicopter pilot to fly him there. (What's the pilot going to do? Say no?)

As it turns out, the storm made the radar transmitters inoperable, so the pilot could fly only visually. That was extremely dangerous because most of the country was socked in with clouds. In the pilot's words: "I couldn't see through the cloud mass, but up ahead, I saw a clear patch of blue and flew in that direction. When I entered the blue patch, I landed here." Wow! God made it so the helicopter had to land in *that* village at *that* very moment! But it gets better . . .

Dr. Morales (the husband) asked if they had any medicines because his village was low on everything. The government had stocked the helicopter full of medical supplies and medicines, so they gave the doctor all he needed to take care of his people. Of course, he asked if Mrs. Morales could fly out with them because the city they were going to had a hospital.

So little Alejandro and his *madre* (mom) were privately escorted directly to the Zacatlan hospital, and she was able to safely deliver a healthy baby girl! *That's prosperity.* That's what having faith and serving a mighty God looks like.

I DARE YOU to quit regarding God as angry at you and always see His unconditional love for you, *even when you mess up.*

> "God wants you to get where God wants
> you to go more than you want to get
> where God wants you to go."
> **- Mark Batterson**

*Dear friend, I pray that you may enjoy
good health and [prosper], even as your
soul is [prospering].*
- 3 John 1:2

May you see prosperity from God's perspective. As the Word says, He owns the cattle on a thousand hills, meaning He owns it all!

REMINDER: We are not victims of our circumstances; children are. We, as adults, are victims of our choices. *Choose wisely. Choose Holy Spirit.*

24

I DON'T WANT TO, LORD

THERE ARE TIMES in believers' lives that the Holy Spirit will prompt us to love an individual that He wants to love *through* us. Whether it's talking to them or offering food, a ride somewhere, clothes, some money, a job, a smile, or a place to stay.

But, for various reasons, our minds just won't go there. First, we are tempted to reason (with ourselves): *This isn't from God.* Maybe we either fear or dislike the person or persons God sends us to. We're like little Jonahs (as we'll see later in this chapter).

We may not feel safe being near them. We reason that cultural differences would cause any attempts to reach them to fail. By doing so, we are forgetting three things: (1) **Matthew 7**, "do to others what you would have them do to you"; (2) **Romans 13**, "owe no one anything but to love one another" (NKJV); and (3) **1 Corinthians 13**, "Love never fails." These three things will encourage us to act to a godly prompting. Remember Jesus said that "'whatever you did [good works] for one of the least of these brothers and sisters of mine, you did for me.'" (**Matthew 25**)

Many of us have experienced the truth of **1 Corinthians 10**, that God won't put us through a temptation that is beyond our grasp to overcome or escape. But can that same assurance be applied to knowing God won't give us a prompting that is outside of our lane (our capacity) to carry out? Consider that:

> God told Gideon to gather men and lead them to attack the Philistine army. Clearly, that was beyond Gideon's ability, but God saw him through it.

> God told Queen Esther to sacrifice her own interests for the posterity of her people. That leading was over the top, yet (through fasting and prayer) she made her entrance to the king, and God used her to save her people.

> God told Abraham to sacrifice his son Isaac. That was beyond the pale of any Hebrew man to attempt, but he took it as far as God would allow it, and God spared Isaac, the child of Promise.

All these promptings, and many more in God's Word, are situations that seemed hopeless or completely not doable, illogical, and even illegal. Yet they were all God's will.

We can look back and see the deliverance, the joy, and the legacy those people would have forfeited if they had not followed the Holy Spirit's prompting: His leading, His fire in their belly.

If we could only learn to replace the word *I* with the word *God*. Then we would find ourselves not saying, "I am not prepared to do this," and see the ridiculousness of saying, "God is not prepared for this." Or . . . "Those young people (over there) have no reason to listen to me," as opposed to: "Those young people have no reason to listen to God." *Oh, really?*

Love never fails. So all we have to do is *apply the love of Jesus* to each of those situations. Real love spans genders, generations, cultures, classes, and attitudes. But we'll never experience that until we do . . . until we submit to the still small voice of the Holy Spirit and not hold back.

So how do we overcome our inhibitions? I'm sorry to say there's no magic pill that gives us the strength and devotion to do what our Master leads us to do (via promptings). Better than magic or medicine is the supernatural work of the Spirit to consume our personal spirit—to change our minds, wills, and emotions.

What could happen when we miss those promptings? The people we could have ministered to (maybe led to Christ) certainly are robbed of a blessing. *But what about us?* Do we incur some kind of loss when we drop the ball and neglect the Holy Spirit's prompting? Better yet, who (in Scripture) said, "I don't want to," to God's leading?

Both Testaments in Scripture give us examples that we can take to the bank. We'll look at two.

Remember I mentioned Jonah (at the beginning)? Let's look at what happened to Jonah in the book named after him. You'll find it between the book of **Obadiah** and the book of **Micah**. The first three verses of **Jonah 1** tell it all: The "word of the Lord" came to Jonah. He got *a word*.

That word was to preach to the Gentile citizens in a town called Nineveh. Instead, Jonah buys a one-way boat ticket going in the totally opposite direction. (Talk about a guy that said, "I don't want to, Lord.") We read that a terrific storm nearly sinks the ship, so the men cast lots to see why the God of Nature is dealing so harshly with them.

The lot falls to Jonah. He confesses to being the cause of God's wrath and tells them to throw him overboard. (Now, here's a guy that is taking responsibility for his own behavior.) Even to the desperate sailors, that was unthinkable, but eventually, they do throw him over. It was that or everybody dies. To the sailors' credit, it was their last resort. To Jonah's credit, he realized it was the first resort . . . the only way to save the others.

During this encounter, the godless, superstitious sailors cried out: "'Please, Lord, do not let us die for taking this man's life. Do not hold us accountable for killing an innocent man, for you, Lord, have done as you pleased." (**Jonah 1**) As soon as Jonah made a big splash, the raging sea was calm. *The result?* "At this the men greatly feared the Lord, and they offered a sacrifice and made vows to him." (**Verse 16**) There was a Holy Spirit revival meeting on the deck of that ship! The men that sailed on to the isle of Tarshish were not the same men that had boarded with Jonah. They had seen the power of God to take their lives and to save them.

God had a sense of humor, along with a sense of purpose. Here, Jonah boarded this ship to avoid preaching to the pagans, and (ultimately) all the pagans onboard have a "come to Jesus" experience that must have stayed with them the rest of their lives. *Hallelujah!* My takeaway is that God can grow His kingdom in spite of our missing His prompting. Our lack of performance doesn't restrict His will.

So, Jonah gets swallowed up by what we would consider a vegan whale. Not a killer whale, but a plankton-centric whale, or "great fish." That swallowing happened before Jonah could drown. Just at the right moment.

From the whale's belly, Jonah prayed: "'When my life was ebbing away, I remembered you, Lord, and my prayer rose to you, to your holy temple. Those who cling to worthless idols turn away from God's love for them. But I, with shouts of grateful praise, will sacrifice to you. What I have vowed I will make good. I will say, "Salvation comes from the Lord."'" (**Jonah 2**)

We have no Scripture indicating Jonah got the joy of knowing that the men who threw him overboard got saved twice—once physically (their lives) and once spiritually (their souls).

OK, so now Jonah is put on dry land, and from that beach, he has a walk of not one, not two, but three days to the "great city" of Nineveh. It must have been the Vegas or Atlantic City of the Mediterranean.

How many days was he in the darkness of the whale's belly? Three. How many days did he get to walk in the open to Nineveh? Three. *Interesting.* In the end, the entire city of Nineveh changed their minds and started to serve the God of the Universe (Jonah's God). *Our God too!*

Remember this all started when Jonah got *a word* from the Lord. After Jonah got that word, a spiritual battle ensued, and Jonah missed his Master's assignment. Rather, he booked a holiday on a Mediterranean island! Instead of Club Med, he got clubbed head, so to speak. However, through God's loving correction, he never got to his "paradise," *and* he didn't drown either. Ultimately, he ended up where God wanted him, and thousands of Ninevite citizens were saved from prophesied destruction *by faith*. That, and the crew of sailors were saved from destruction *by sight*. (They saw and knew they were all going to die.)

Listen, Jonah didn't fear failure (in Nineveh). He feared success. His experience shows us that even when we go left and God's assignment is to go right, God will bring us to the right and win (on both sides) because He's God. He's invested in us. He knows the outcome before the beginning. He's for us and not against us. The Holy Spirit will never ever fail us.

In the New Testament, who said, "I don't want to, Lord," to a directive of God by the prompting of the Holy Spirit? Perhaps Saul of Tarsus fits that mold. Surely the Holy Spirt was knocking on the door of his heart (from his youth), but in his zeal, he didn't respond. He was too busy earning Brownie points with the Hebrew leaders to hear from God. He was an upwardly mobile Jew.

In fact, Saul was a bounty hunter on an expedition to capture believers in Damascus and drag them back to

Jerusalem when Jesus struck him blind. That was Saul's ticket to darkness. **Acts 9** reveals that, like Jonah, Saul was in darkness for three days. Both men fasted for three days. *Why?*

Because they knew they needed to change their mind and course-correct to get (and stay on) God's path. God knows we're not perfect. He gives us permission to fail. But when we do fail, it should not lead us to worldly depression and defeat. Not at all! Like Jonah and Saul, we *get to* experience Godly sorrow in those moments. *That's the difference!*

I DARE YOU to answer God's promptings by submitting to *a word* from the Holy Spirit as many as He chooses to give you in life.

> "When we fear man or man's rejection of the gospel more than we fear God, then we are ignoring the prompting of the Holy Spirit."
> **– Jack Wellman**

> *Although the Lord gives you the bread of adversity and the water of affliction, your teachers will be hidden no more; with your own eyes you will see them.*

*Whether you turn to the right or the left,
your ears will hear a voice behind you,
saying, "This is the way; walk in it."*
– Isaiah 30:20-21

May you gain victory over any resistant spirit that lures you away from faith and obedience to the impulses of the Holy Spirit.

REMINDER: We are not victims of our circumstances; children are. We, as adults, are victims of our choices. *Choose wisely. Choose Holy Spirit.*

25

THE WIND BENEATH OUR WINGS

JESUS SAID, "THUS, BY THEIR FRUIT you will recognize them." (**Matthew 7**) He was talking about false prophets, the "fake news" spreaders of that day. The fact of the matter is that His litmus test applies to every one of us. We are all known by our fruits: our actions, our character, and our behaviors.

Have you ever done something that you never thought you could do? Maybe it was solving an equation, speaking in public, bench pressing a higher weight, or having a baby. Afterwards, you said to yourself: "I didn't know I had that in me!" (Not the baby, of course.) There was a "fruit," a capacity, in you that even you didn't know was there until your actions revealed it.

I have a friend who was a teenager on the beach in San Clemente, California. By his own admission, he was not an especially good swimmer and would NEVER go swimming without wearing his nose plugs to keep water out of his nose. One day, he and his buddy were lying on the sand (facing the surf) and talking with a couple of bikini-clad girls when (all of a sudden) an old lady that had waded into the Pacific was being swept away and was in obvious distress about that—waving her arms.

For a second, the teen guys looked at each other, as if to say, *Somebody's got to help her,* and then they got up and ran as fast as they could into the ocean. They were able to (mostly) wade out to her, lock arms, and carry this poor, overweight soul back to dry land. They went from beach bums to heroes in less than five minutes.

What happened there? A circumstance (that they could not control) exposed something in them they didn't know even existed. The thought of not going into the water without nose plugs never occurred to Dave nor his buddy Mark. The immediacy of the need far exceeded the luxury of worrying about possible outcomes or imperfections in their methods.

They had ZERO rescue training, but what those two kids did with that woman (that they could have never carried alone) was a textbook rescue.

With two locked arms, they formed a seat for her lower body to sit on, and the other two locked arms were placed across her back to hold her torso upright. This took mere seconds to form. There was nothing immodest in handling her, and doing it that way maintained her dignity (and didn't give anybody nightmares going forward).

What was a surprise to the guys was no surprise to the Holy Spirit. Of all the miles of coastline, the Lord arranged these two guys to be in the old lady's rescue zone. There is no logical reason that, with no equipment, Mark and Dave got that lady out in a New York minute.

She's alive because those guys were where God wanted them to be. She's alive because they didn't look at each other and say, *Not me!* They were willing to play the role God gave them the opportunity to play. Did they *have to* plunge into the water to save her? No, they *got to* plunge into the water to save her.

They didn't have preparation for this event, but they had proximity, purpose, and (ultimately) performance that rescued the helpless woman. They can't take credit for where they were lying in the sand (proximity). They can't take credit for the flawless actions that truly saved the frightened woman (performance). They only thing they deserve mention for is their willingness to participate in God's will (purpose). It wasn't her time to die, and it was God's intent that she be rescued.

I hope you join me in personalizing this true story and rest in knowing that God places us where He wants us to be so that we are in proximity of something He's going to do.

I hope you know that your performance is more on the Holy Spirit than it is on you and, when the time comes, you will be used of God to do something exceedingly, abundantly in the life (or lives) of those who aren't supposed to die that day or get evicted that day or commit suicide that day or have an abortion that day. May the immediacy of the need far exceed your luxury of worrying about possible outcomes or imperfections in your methods.

In your future reading in the Scriptures (which I trust will be soon), try to observe who's doing or saying what . . . and whether they are in the Spirit or in the flesh. For instance, in **Matthew 16**, we hear the disciple Peter making a wonderful confession that Jesus is "the Messiah, the Son of the Living God."

Jesus so much as declares that Peter's words were Spirit-inspired. A mere five verses later, Peter goes from confessor to rebuker, as Jesus had just prophesied His death and three-day resurrection: "'Never, Lord!' [Peter] said. 'This shall not happen to you!'" (**Matthew 16**)

Now, you be the judge. Was Peter speaking in the Spirit (again) or in the flesh? Jesus discerned that right away when He said out loud to Peter, "'Get behind me, Satan! . . . you do not have in mind the concerns of God.'" (**Verse 23**)

Question: Was Peter demon-possessed? No. Jesus wasn't talking to Peter. He was talking to a lying spirit, using Peter as a mouthpiece. There's a difference between talking *to* and talking *through*. In **Matthew 16**, the Holy Spirit is talking *through* Peter, and Jesus is talking *to* him. In **verse 22**, the devil is talking *through* Peter and Jesus is talking *to* the devil.

That is why James makes the observation of our human tongues: "With the tongue we praise our Lord and Father, and with it we curse human beings, who have been made in God's likeness. Out of the same mouth come praise and cursing. My brothers and sisters, this should not be." **(James 3)**

We know that whatever Jesus said was inspired and approved by the Father. When the disciples of Jesus were forbidding mothers to bring Him their children, causing Him to say, "'Let the little children come to me, and do not hinder them,'" He was in the Spirit. **(Luke 18)** When Jesus told the woman (caught in adultery), "'Then neither do I condemn you,'" He was in the Spirit. **(John 8)** When He overturned the tables of the money-changers in the Temple, while saying, "'My house will be called a house of prayer, but you are making it a den of robbers,'" He was in the Spirit. **(Matthew 21)** When he told the scribes, Pharisees, and chief priests, "'You belong to your father, the devil, and you want to carry out your father's desires,'" He was in the Spirit. **(John 8)**

For sure, Stephen was in the Spirit in **Acts 7**, when he schooled his detractors in the things of the Lord. So much so, that their wicked hearts were enraged at him exposing their iniquity and failure to truly follow the God of Abraham, Isaac, and Jacob.

Philip was in the Spirit when he expounded the *Who behind the what* in **Isaiah 53**. That was where the Ethiopian eunuch was reading in the Scriptures when Philip appeared alongside him in the road.

Philip didn't fuss about how to share the Good News with the Ethiopian. Stephen did not prepare a PowerPoint presentation for his accusers. They *let go and let God* speak through them. The Holy Spirit was the wind beneath their wings—lifting them up, giving them an opportunity to be available to preach or teach or give or simply demonstrate what God designed them to do in that moment.

We can be sure that Ananias in **Acts 5**, *was not* in the Spirit when he misled the apostle Peter at what price he had sold his land. And equally sure, in **Acts 9**, when another Ananias *was in* the Spirit when he said to the Hebrew bounty hunter, "'Brother Saul, the Lord—Jesus, who appeared to you on the road as you were coming here—has sent me so that you may see again and be filled with the Holy Spirit.'" It was Saul's moment to soar. How could Ananias prophesy to a man that he feared?

By letting go (of his fear) and letting God speak through him.

Isaiah 40: "those who hope in the Lord will renew their strength. They will soar on wings like eagles." The Holy Spirit is always poised to be the wind beneath our wings, but to benefit from Him, our wings must be open to Him. If we keep our wings (our thoughts, desires, expectations) too close to ourselves, we cannot soar with the current of the Spirit to take us where we need to go.

A 2020 study, published in the journal *Proceedings of the National Academy of Sciences*, reports that Andean condors can soar for hours and up to distances of one hundred miles without a single flap of their wings! What a lesson these birds teach us—that we, in the Spirit with our wings spread, can be transported and effortlessly align with God's will.

Scientists that study birds recognize the two types of flight as flapping flight and soaring flight. As humans, even as kids, we experienced the difference between pedaling a bike uphill (flapping flight) and coasting downhill (soaring flight). Even though it's not a perfect analogy, we can relate to pedaling through life on our own efforts or coasting through life by the momentum of the Holy Spirit. *Which life do you want?*

I DARE YOU to stop pedaling up the hills of your life and ask Jesus to strengthen you in the inner man (or woman) and open your wings to allow the Spirit to soar you through every challenge and every opportunity.

> "Be like the bird, who
> Halting in his flight
> On limb too slight
> Feels it give way beneath him
> Yet sings
> Knowing he hath wings."
> **– Victor Hugo**

> *"Be on your guard; you will be handed over to the local councils and be flogged in the synagogues. . . . But when they arrest you, do not worry about what to say or how to say it. At that time you will be given what to say, for it will not be you speaking, but the Spirit of your Father speaking through you."*
> **– Matthew 10:17, 19-20**

May your wings be extended to the Spirit when you feel like it and when you don't.

REMINDER: We are not victims of our circumstances; children are. We, as adults, are victims of our choices. *Choose wisely. Choose Holy Spirit.*

26

QUENCH YOUR THIRST, NOT THE SPIRIT

LIVING UNDER THE INFLUENCE of the Holy Spirit is the best way to live, but it does squarely put us in the enemy's crosshairs as he wants to quench the Spirit's leading in our lives.

In **1 Thessalonians 5**, it says, "Do not quench the Spirit." Synonyms for *quench* include extinguish (like putting out a fire), smother (like being suffocated), and stifle (like diminishing someone's passion by silly arguments and distractions).

Next, the antonyms: ignite (like starting a flame and kindling it to keep it going) and stimulate (feeding one's passion for Jesus). Now, ask yourself: *What is happening in my church? What is happening in my home? Are they places of igniting or smothering?*

So *what quenches the Spirit?* Well, I could make a list of things, like gossip, envy, pride, lust, greed, legalism, et cetera. *What good would that do?* We know that already, and we are either OK with those things in our life or not. That's focusing on behavior modification, and that's not what any of my books are about.

How about we focus on igniting? What ignites us to live under the influence of the Holy Spirit? You may remember singer/pianist Keith Green. Two lines of the many touching lyrics of the song "Oh Lord, You're Beautiful" go like this: "Oh, Lord, please light the fire / That once burned bright and clear."

Those are beautiful lyrics to that song. However, that "fire" is not an emotion, something we manufacture. That fire is the Holy Spirit, and we already have that fire within us!

We all have a personal spirit, and believers have the fire, but at times, we can't feel its warmth. There's no glow, so we assume the Spirit of God is not within us. But He is. *So how do we get that warmth back?*

Let me ask you: How did you get the fire, glow, and warmth in the first place? Was it by an emotional feeling or a faith-induced fact of life? Did it come by your *preference* or by God's *promise* (to give you a Comforter)? His was a promise made and a promise kept. *End of story.*

The moment I stop feeling the warmth of God's fire in me is the moment I need to get out my Faith card and let that faith override my doubts and fears (about losing what God has given me). Our lane is to merely place ourselves under the shadow of the Almighty. He takes care of the rest. That's His lane.

It is Jesus's doing—baptizing us in His Holy Spirit. John the Baptist told us, plainly, in **Matthew 3**: "I baptize you with water for repentance. But after me comes one who is more powerful than I, whose sandals I am not worthy to carry. He will baptize you with the Holy Spirit and with fire."

Let's not overcomplicate this truth: the Holy Spirit draws (baptizes) us to Jesus, and Jesus baptizes us in the Holy Spirit. (There's the fire! It's always within us.) There is life in that God-ordained continuum.

That has always been the Lord's plan. At the same time, let's be honest; emotions do get in the way. Things like fear and guilt assault us and can quench our personal fire for God, our "want to." So we address these energy-taking emotions head-on.

As living under the influence of the Holy Spirit, what do we do when we feel guilty? *We go to the Word* and let God's Word define whether we are guilty or not. For that, we'll look at **Romans 8** again.

Before we go there, let's lay some powerful foundation from **Hebrews 10**. I'm going to have you read it through as I read it. First, we'll see the forest. Next, we'll walk through the trees. Finally, we'll look back for a summary or takeaway. *Ready?*

Hebrews 10:1. "The law is only a shadow of the good things that are coming—not the realities themselves. For this reason it can never, by the same sacrifices repeated endlessly year after year, make perfect those who draw near to worship."

I read all the words, just as you did. Next, I go back and mine the "trees," the key nouns, action verbs, and modifiers:

Hebrews 10:1 (with emphasis added). "**The law** is only a shadow of the good things that are coming—not the realities themselves. For this reason, it **can never**, by the same sacrifices repeated endlessly year after year, **make perfect** those who draw near to worship."

There it is! Almost in code: *The Law can never make perfect!*

OK, Mike, so what?

Let's continue to read verses 2 and 3:

Hebrews 10:2. "Otherwise, would they not have stopped being offered? For the worshippers would have been cleansed once for all, and would no longer have felt **guilty** for their sins." (Emphasis added.)

Hebrews 10: 3. "But those sacrifices are an annual **reminder of sins**." (Emphasis added.)

To summarize: *The Law can never make perfect because there's an awareness and a reminder of your sins and mine.* Under the Law, you're aware of sin, and you're reminded of sin. What the Spirit says to us is: *With Jesus and what He did, there's no more consciousness of sin, no more awareness of your sin over and over and over again.* Why?

Because the debt has been **paid in full**. The account has been settled! The enemy will send his bill collectors to us saying, "You owe, you owe," but we don't. We rebuke those "collectors" in Jesus's name. We do this out loud because that lets *them know* that *we know* the bill has been paid and there will never ever be a debt of sin on us again. *Hallelujah!*

Continuing in **Hebrews 10**:

Hebrews 10:14. "For by one sacrifice **he has made perfect** forever those who are being made holy." (That's us! And "has made" is *past tense.* Emphasis added.)

Hebrews 10:15. "The Holy Spirit also testifies to us about this. First He says:"

Hebrews 10:16. "'This is the covenant I will make with them after that time, says the Lord. I will put my laws in their hearts, and I will write them on their minds.'" [We're talking fulfilled laws (in Christ), not unfulfilled laws.]

Hebrews 10:17. "Then he adds: 'Their sins and lawless deeds **I will remember no more.**'" (Emphasis added.)

Hebrews 10:18. "And where these have been forgiven, sacrifice for sin is no longer necessary." (*Yessss!*)

You can see why I can't abide feeling guilty or condemned. Guilt and condemnation are like a pair of gloves. If you have one, you'll have the other.

At the beginning of this chapter, I said that when we find ourselves feeling guilty, we look to **Romans 8**, so let's look again at **verse 1**: "Therefore, there is now no condemnation for those who are in Christ Jesus."

You feel guilty only when there's condemnation. If you're not condemned, you can't feel guilty; it's impossible! So there's a condemnation that goes with guilt, and there's guilt only when you are aware of your sin, and you're aware of your sin only if you are under the Law. NEWSFLASH: We're not under the Law.

"And if the **Spirit of him** who raised Jesus from the dead **is living in you**, he who raised **[Jesus]** from the dead will also give life to your mortal bodies because of his Spirit who lives in you." (**Verse 11**, emphasis added) Wow. What a great plan. What a great promise. *What a great God!*

OK, Mike, I can begin to grasp that the Spirit who raised Jesus from the dead lives in me, but why do I catch myself quenching the Spirit? What drives that kind of thinking?

One word: conscience.

My friend Lee Bramlett (author of *Holy Justice Holy Blood*) described *conscience* fully to me, as he points us to Adam in the garden and how he was created in right standing before Almighty God:

> Adam's nakedness in the garden revealed his right standing with God. He was innocent . . . righteous, and had nothing to hide. His shame came when he sinned. Now, he had something to hide. Now, he was afraid.
>
> When God asked: "'Who told you that you were naked?"' It was like the moment in a crime story—when the investigator says to the person in custody: "How did you know a knife was used in the murder? That was never released to the press." The presence of knowledge (of the knife) exposed the killer.
>
> In the same way, Adam's awareness, or knowledge, of being naked ("'I was naked and ashamed so I hid"') revealed the sinner himself. *Who had told Adam he was naked?* It was not Satan, nor was it God. Adam had told himself, and at that moment, the conscience was born. . . .
>
> . . . Adam tasted of the tree of the Knowledge of Good and Evil. He was separated from God and now he had his own moral compass, born of this separation. That is why every man, woman, and child is born with a conscience in a fallen state.

The Holy Spirit does not speak to a man or a woman's fallen conscience because it's all screwed up! What my conscience thinks is right, may be wrong. What my conscience thinks is wrong, may be right. The Holy Spirit reveals everything Jesus said to us. It's the Word of God; that's our consciousness, the pure Word of God.

That's what the Holy Spirit is saying: *Feed your spirit with the Word of God, unlock the Kingdom power of your soul in prayer, and with your soul, direct your body to keep in step with the Spirit.*

Let's take one last look at **verse 14** of **Hebrews 10**. *What's it say?* "For by one sacrifice **he** has **made perfect forever** those who are being made holy." (Emphasis added) So, by one sacrifice, He has made perfect. Brothers and sisters, that's a past tense. We *were* made perfect, not *are being made perfect.* End of story.

Because we were made perfect, we are fully sanctified. We're not born holy; we're made holy. We're set apart. God set us apart, and when He set us apart, He said: *You're a new creation in Christ Jesus. And now that you're a new creation, you're perfect. You are perfect in Christ. You are fully sanctified. Now, walk that out.*

But we get stuck in our soul, and our soul becomes the god we serve—our mind, our will, our emotions, and our conscience. That's Satan's playground. He can't touch your spirit. It's impossible. No, he can't touch our spirit, but he can play with our soul (which he does every day). Then, we start believing what our soul says to us and not what God says. **Stop that!**

Lee Bramlett points out that, at conversion, "the Holy Spirit is at work in the human heart. And if the human heart stays grateful, we'll rest in knowing (not just believing) that even if our conscience condemns us, we have been set free by the very Judge that we will all stand before."

"If our hearts condemn us, we know that God is greater than our hearts [conscience], and he knows everything." (**1 John 3**) "The one who keeps God's commands lives in him, and he in them. And this is how we know that he lives in us: We know it by the Spirit he gave us." (**Verse 24**)

So, when doubts want to quench our living under the influence, we look at the key witnesses as revealed in **1 John 5**: "There is the one who came by water and blood—Jesus Christ. He did not come by water only, but by water and blood. And it is the Spirit who testifies because the Spirit is the truth. For there are three that testify: the Spirit, the water and the blood; and the three are in agreement."

Finally, let's recap the questions you read in chapter 1: *What is the role of the Holy Spirit?*

There are multiple roles. Holy Spirit's key role for humanity is to *glorify Jesus.* Holy Spirit's main role for unbelievers is to *convince them of sin and baptize them to Jesus.* Holy Spirit's main role for believers is to *bring to our remembrance that we are in right standing before God.* He convinces us of our right standing. We were already convinced of our sin; that brought us to Jesus. Now, we just need to be convinced of our right standing, which is the role of the Holy Spirit.

How does He work in our day-to-day life?

Well, that was explained (above). He guides us. He comforts us. He helps us apply the Word to our life situations by bringing the right verse or verses to our attention at the right time. Also, **Romans 8** says He prays for us when we don't know what to pray.

Do we pray to Him?

That's kind of a trick question. We don't pray, "Our Holy Spirit, who art in Heaven . . ." At the same time, the Holy Spirit is the Spirit of God, and God is Spirit. So I would say that praying to God is praying to the Spirit. Praying *in* the Spirit looks at *how* we pray (perhaps in tongues or in song). *Whom* we pray to is another matter. Jesus taught a prayer that begins: "Our Father."

Should we honor Him and worship Him?

As I said before, the Holy Spirit is God. Unlike Jesus, He was never "God in the flesh" because He is God in the Spirit. That's the Holy Spirit's lane. Yes, to worship God is to worship and praise the Son and the Holy Spirit. It's OK to sing to the Spirit and communicate with Him and by Him. He has your back.

I DARE YOU to ready yourself for the Holy Spirit's assignments and put on the full armor of God every day as you walk in the Spirit. The apostle Paul described the armor in **Ephesians 6**: the belt of truth, the breastplate of righteousness, feet adorned with the gospel of peace, the shield of faith, the helmet of salvation, and the sword of the Spirit (the Word of God).

> "When a person comes to Christ he has a new relationship with his conscience just as he has a new relationship with the Law."
> **– Dietrich Bonhoeffer**

> Submit yourselves, then, to God. Resist the devil, and he will flee from you.
> **– James 4:7**

May you always remember that the sacrifice for your sins has already been made. It is a sacrifice not in the distant future but in the distant, yet relevant, past.

REMINDER: We are not victims of our circumstances; children are. We, as adults, are victims of our choices. *Choose wisely. Choose Holy Spirit.*